STANLEY THORNES

infant RE

Year1/P2

TEACHER'S RESOURCE BOOK

Louis Fidge and
Christine Moorcroft

STANLEY THORNES
CHELTENHAM

Text © Louis Fidge and Christine Moorcroft 1997

The right of Louis Fidge and Christine Moorcroft to be identified as the authors of this work has been asserted by them in accordance with the Copyright, Designs and Patents Act 1988.

Acknowledgements:
'My Baby Brother', Mary Ann Hoberman and 'Our Family Comes from around the World', Mary Ann Hoberman, from *Fathers, Mothers, Sisters, Brothers* by Mary Ann Hoberman and Marilyn Hafner, text © 1991 Mary Ann Hoberman, illustrations © 1991 Marilyn Hafner, by permission of Little Brown Inc. 'Think of a World without any Flowers', Doreen Newport, by permission of Stainer and Bell Ltd. 'The Sun Wakes Up', © John Rice, from *Rockets and Quasars* (Aten Press, 1984). 'Weather', Lucy Coats, from *First Rhymes*, first published in the UK by Orchard Books, a division of the Watts Publishing Group, 96 Leonard Street, London, EC2A 4RH. 'Who Put the Colours in the Rainbow', Paul Booth, by permission of Matthew Booth. 'The Swan', adapted from the story by Dorothy Vause and Liz Beaumont, from the *Junior Assembly Book*, Stanley Thornes Publishers. 'What It's Worth', by permission of CEM.

Poster illustrations by: 'At Home', Martin Sookias; 'My Family', Martin Sookias; 'My Day', John Crawford Fraser; 'Belonging', Martin Sookias; 'Hurt no Living Thing', earthworm © Andre Maslennikov/Still Pictures, worm farm, Sweden, Uppsala, Haus Agrell; 'The Seasons', photographs © Denis Bringard/Still Pictures; 'Holi', John Crawford Fraser; 'Easter', Andrea Mantegna, *The Maries at the Sepulchre* (panel from a series), reproduced by courtesy of the Trustees, The National Gallery, London; 'The Bible', Arundel 83 f. 14 Stags and birds, English, Arundel Psalter © British Library, London/Bridgeman Art Library; 'Jesus Calms the Storm', Celia Hart; 'Messages all around Us', Peter Bull Art Studio; 'The Qur'an', Martin Sookias.

All rights reserved. The copyright holders authorise ONLY users of *Stanley Thornes Infant RE Year 1* to make photocopies or stencil duplicates of the photocopiable worksheets for their own or their classes' immediate use within the teaching context. No other rights are granted without permission in writing from the publishers or under licence from the Copyright Licensing Agency Limited. Further details of such licences (for reprographic reproduction) may be obtained from the Copyright Licensing Agency Limited of 90 Tottenham Court Road, London W1P 0LP. Copy by any other means or for any other purpose is strictly prohibited without prior written consent from the copyright holders. Application for such permission should be addressed to the publishers.

First published in 1997 by
Stanley Thornes Publishers Ltd
Ellenborough House
Wellington Street
Cheltenham
GL50 1YW

99 00 01 02 03\ 10 9 8 7 6 5 4 3 2

A catalogue record for this book is available from the British Library

ISBN 0-7487-3042-7

Designed by Penny Mills
Illustrated by Chris Masters
Cover illustration by Alex Ayliffe

Printed in Great Britain by Antony Rowe Ltd., Chippenham, Wiltshire

Contents

Introduction 4

Unit 1 Myself. 8

Unit 2 New Life. 30

Unit 3 Special Books 52

Extra Photocopy Sheets 74

Poems, Songs and Prayers 78

Stories 81

Extra Background Information 99

Introduction

Stanley Thornes Infant RE provides a complete, self-contained, structured programme for teaching religious education throughout Years 1 and 2/P2 and 3.

The scheme is based on the recommendations of the School Curriculum and Assessment Authority (SCAA) (1994) and is compatible with locally agreed syllabuses and the Scottish 5–14 guidelines. It complies with the Education Reform Act (1988) which requires that religious education should '...reflect the fact that the religious traditions in Great Britain are in the main Christian, while taking account of teachings and practices of other principal religions represented in Great Britain ...' Following SCAA recommendations the six faiths addressed are: Buddhism, Christianity, Hinduism, Islam, Judaism and Sikhism, with the emphasis on Christianity. It takes into account the fact that most infant schools will choose which of these faiths to include and give priority to in their religious education schemes.

In addition to learning about religions the scheme offers opportunities to learn from religions; this supports the promotion of children's spiritual, moral and cultural development.

To help non-specialist teachers and to save the teacher's time the relevant background information for each religious topic is always provided, as are stories, poems, songs and prayers, where appropriate.

Stanley Thornes Infant RE is designed to help pupils to:

◆ develop knowledge and understanding of Christianity and the other main religions of Great Britain;

◆ understand the ways in which beliefs, values and traditions influence people, communities and culture;

◆ use the teachings of the major faiths to inform thoughtful judgements about religious and moral issues;

◆ develop social, moral, cultural and spiritual awareness by:

- becoming aware of the fundamental questions of life which are raised by the experiences of people and considering them in the light of religious teachings;
- in considering these questions, referring to the teachings and practices of the religions which they have studied;
- thinking about their own beliefs, values and experiences against the background of their learning about different religions;

◆ become increasingly positive in their attitudes towards others, being able to respect their beliefs and values and develop the ability to live in a multi-faith society.

The introduction to each unit shows the religious focus of each lesson and gives an overview of how the six major faiths are addressed. Reflecting the way in which religious education is taught in most infant schools, the approach of the scheme is topic-based, with many opportunities for discussion of 'general' topics which are not tied to just one religion, for example, personal identity, family and celebrating. It recognises that many schools address the Christian festivals, Christmas and Easter, each year; these appear in both Books 1 and 2, but with built-in progression, enabling teachers to build on and develop from the children's previous learning.

As required by the Education Reform Act (1988) the scheme presents religious education in a way which supports teachers in developing children's understanding of different faiths without attempting to inculcate a particular religious belief in the children. It recognises that the children who learn from it, and their teachers, are from a range of faith backgrounds or none at all.

TERMINOLOGY

The terminology used in *Stanley Thornes Infant RE* is in line with the specific spellings and usages recommended by SCAA. However, there may be local variations to these and schools will need to be sensitive to local and regional conventions. In all the pupils' material, and on the first mention in the teacher's material, the name of the Prophet Muhammad is followed by the initials 'pbuh'. This is the written abbreviation of the words 'Peace be upon him', which are always spoken after Muhammad's name by Muslims, as a mark of respect. Again, schools will need to be sensitive to this practice, and also to any variations of this phrase which may be in use locally.

ORGANISATION

Stanley Thornes Infant RE provides two 112-page teacher's books, each of which is supported by 12 full-colour posters. It is appreciated that no published scheme can possibly address the individual needs of every school. With this in mind, the books are designed to be as flexible as possible. The units may be interchanged with one another; the lessons within each unit are self-contained, and so the sequence of lessons may be altered to suit the needs of the school. The scheme takes account of the fact that some schools have mixed-age classes; the differentiated learning outcomes are particularly useful in these schools. They are also intended to encourage teachers to develop each child's learning to the full.

Each book is organised into three units (one per term), followed by a resources section which offers stories and additional background information. Each unit has a brief introduction setting out its contents and indicating its intended learning outcomes.

STANLEY THORNES
infant RE

Year 1/ P2
Myself
New Life
Special Books

Year 2/ P3
Special Times
Special People
Special Places

A unit consists of ten one-hour 'lessons' (easily divisible into shorter sections) each of which consists of lesson plan notes faced by a photocopy sheet. The teacher's pages have been designed to facilitate ease of use, with clear and consistent headings.

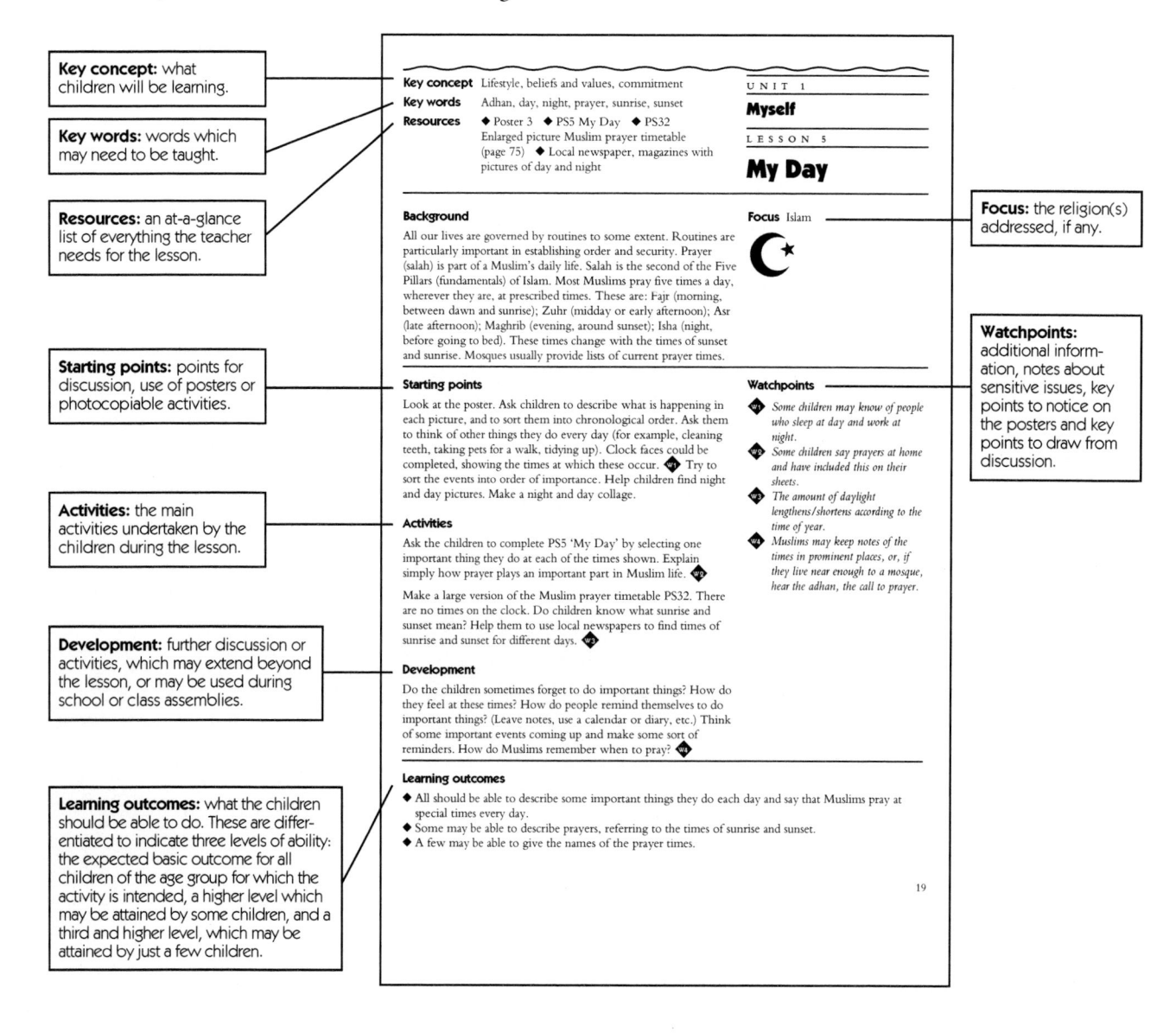

Key concept: what children will be learning.

Key words: words which may need to be taught.

Resources: an at-a-glance list of everything the teacher needs for the lesson.

Starting points: points for discussion, use of posters or photocopiable activities.

Activities: the main activities undertaken by the children during the lesson.

Development: further discussion or activities, which may extend beyond the lesson, or may be used during school or class assemblies.

Learning outcomes: what the children should be able to do. These are differentiated to indicate three levels of ability: the expected basic outcome for all children of the age group for which the activity is intended, a higher level which may be attained by some children, and a third and higher level, which may be attained by just a few children.

Key concept Lifestyle, beliefs and values, commitment
Key words Adhan, day, night, prayer, sunrise, sunset
Resources ◆ Poster 3 ◆ PS5 My Day ◆ PS32 Enlarged picture Muslim prayer timetable (page 75) ◆ Local newspaper, magazines with pictures of day and night

UNIT 1
Myself
LESSON 5
My Day

Background
All our lives are governed by routines to some extent. Routines are particularly important in establishing order and security. Prayer (salah) is part of a Muslim's daily life. Salah is the second of the Five Pillars (fundamentals) of Islam. Most Muslims pray five times a day, wherever they are, at prescribed times. These are: Fajr (morning, between dawn and sunrise); Zuhr (midday or early afternoon); Asr (late afternoon); Maghrib (evening, around sunset); Isha (night, before going to bed). These times change with the times of sunset and sunrise. Mosques usually provide lists of current prayer times.

Focus Islam

Starting points
Look at the poster. Ask children to describe what is happening in each picture, and to sort them into chronological order. Ask them to think of other things they do every day (for example, cleaning teeth, taking pets for a walk, tidying up). Clock faces could be completed, showing the times at which these occur. Try to sort the events into order of importance. Help children find night and day pictures. Make a night and day collage.

Watchpoints
- Some children may know of people who sleep at day and work at night.
- Some children say prayers at home and have included this on their sheets.
- The amount of daylight lengthens/shortens according to the time of year.
- Muslims may keep notes of the times in prominent places, or, if they live near enough to a mosque, hear the adhan, the call to prayer.

Activities
Ask the children to complete PS5 'My Day' by selecting one important thing they do at each of the times shown. Explain simply how prayer plays an important part in Muslim life.

Make a large version of the Muslim prayer timetable PS32. There are no times on the clock. Do children know what sunrise and sunset mean? Help them to use local newspapers to find times of sunrise and sunset for different days.

Development
Do the children sometimes forget to do important things? How do they feel at these times? How do people remind themselves to do important things? (Leave notes, use a calendar or diary, etc.) Think of some important events coming up and make some sort of reminders. How do Muslims remember when to pray?

Learning outcomes
◆ All should be able to describe some important things they do each day and say that Muslims pray at special times every day.
◆ Some may be able to describe prayers, referring to the times of sunrise and sunset.
◆ A few may be able to give the names of the prayer times.

Focus: the religion(s) addressed, if any.

Watchpoints: additional information, notes about sensitive issues, key points to notice on the posters and key points to draw from discussion.

ASSESSMENT AND RECORDING

England and Wales

The 'end of Key Stage statements of attainment' suggested by SCAA are adopted here as the criteria by which children's learning should be assessed:

Learning about religions (AT1)
Pupils recognise and describe people, objects, symbols, places and events encountered [in the programme of study], and remember the outlines of stories. They talk or write about a religion, or an aspect of

religion, linking some of the key people, objects, places and events. They identify the religions to which these belong, and show awareness that some features, for example festivals, are characteristic of more than one religion. They suggest meanings for religious symbols, stories and language: for example, God as Father.

Learning from religion (AT2)
Pupils respond to spiritual or religious aspects of stories in the light of their own experience and thoughts. They show understanding that some questions in life are difficult to answer. They recognise good and bad examples set by characters in stories and by those around them. They show awareness that some things are right and some are wrong, and relate the moral issues encountered in their daily lives to religious teachings.

The learning outcomes of each lesson are linked to these statements and provide a basis for completing the photocopiable Pupil Record Sheet (page 106).

Scotland

'Learning about religions', above, equates to the 5-14 attainment outcomes 'Christianity' and 'Other World Relgions'.
'Learning from religion', above, equates to the 5-14 'Personal Search'.

STANLEY THORNES
infant RE

UNIT 1

Myself

INTRODUCTION

Who am I? How do I feel? What makes me special?

Key questions such as these are important to every individual.

This unit is designed to help children understand themselves as individuals and members of society better. Children are encouraged to express their thoughts and feelings about themselves and others. They learn how religious beliefs shape and influence the lives of individuals and communities.

Unit 1 – Overview

Lesson	Contents	Key Concepts	Religious Focus
1	**Who am I?** 'Who am I?' is one of life's big questions. ◆ What is my place in the overall scheme of things? ◆ How am I the same as/different from others? ◆ What makes me special?	Ultimate questions, lifestyle	General/ Sikhism
2	**How do I Feel?** Learning about and understanding our feelings is important if we are to be able to relate appropriately to others. ◆ What sort of feelings do we experience? ◆ How do people express their feelings? ◆ How do we know what others are feeling?	Ultimate questions, lifestyle	General
3	**At Home** Homes are formative influences on our values, attitudes and belief systems. The example of a Jewish family celebrating Shabbat is used to emphasise this. ◆ Why is a home important? ◆ How do Jewish families celebrate Shabbat? ◆ How is this important to them?	Lifestyle, belonging, commitment	Judaism
4	**My Family** Family units vary enormously in composition and culture. Hindus place a lot of emphasis on family relationships. ◆ Why are families important? ◆ How do Hindus emphasise family bonds? ◆ Do we have to live together to be a 'family'?	Lifestyle, belonging commitment	Hinduism

Lesson	Contents	Key Concepts	Religious Focus
5	**My Day** All our lives are governed by routines to some extent. Prayer is very much a part of a Muslim's daily routine. ◆ What sort of things do we do every day? ◆ Can we identify regular daily routines in our lives? ◆ What role does prayer have in a Muslim's daily life?	Lifestyle, commitment, beliefs and values	Islam
6	**My Friends** The story of Ruth and Naomi is used to bring out important aspects of friendship. ◆ What sort of things do friends do together? ◆ What qualities typify friendship? ◆ What can we learn from the story about friendship?	Lifestyle, commitment	Judaism/ Christianity
7	**Jesus' Friends** Jesus chose some special friends, his disciples, to help him with his earthly ministry. ◆ Why did Jesus choose some special friends? ◆ Who were they? ◆ What can we learn from the friends Jesus chose?	Authority, inspiration, belonging, commitment	Christianity
8	**Thinking of Others** In most major religions the belief in the need to think about others is clearly expressed. The Islamic belief in zakah and the provision of food at Sikh langars is explored. ◆ Why is it important to think of others? ◆ What is the Muslim belief in zakah? ◆ What is a langar for in a Sikh temple?	Beliefs, values, lifestyle, commitment	Islam/ Sikhism
9	**Belonging** We all belong to different groups. The Five Ks are a reminder of what it means to belong to the Sikh faith. ◆ What sort of groups do we belong to? ◆ How does an adult male Sikh dress? ◆ What do these clothes signify?	Lifestyle, belonging, symbolism	Sikhism
10	**A Special Baby – The Christmas Story** Christians celebrate the birth of Christ at Christmas. To them, Jesus is a very special person. ◆ In what ways are all babies special? ◆ What are the details of the Christmas Story? ◆ Why is Jesus special to Christians?	Authority, inspiration, beliefs, values	Christianity

I am special

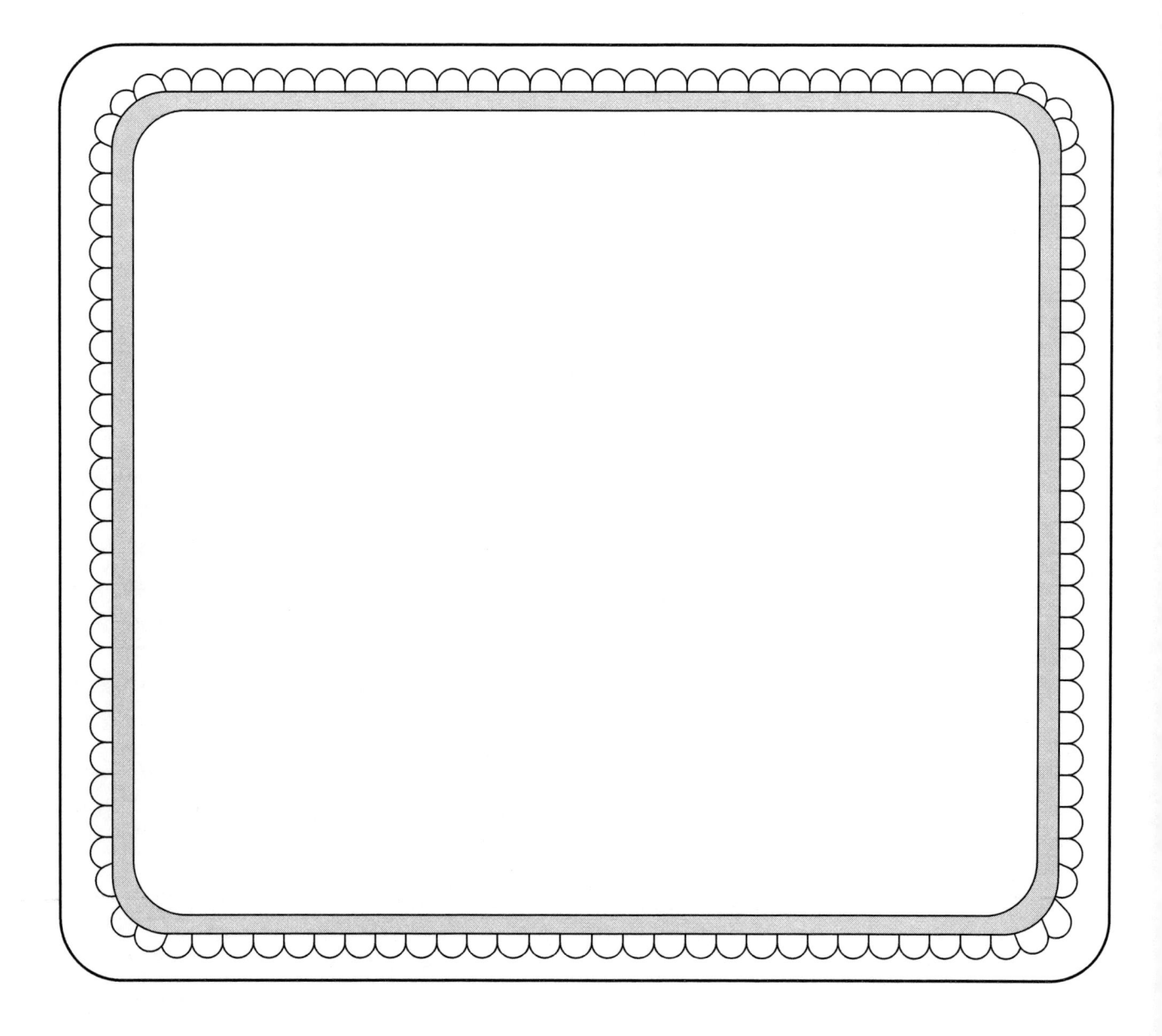

My name is _____

I am _____

I can _____

I like _____

Key concept Ultimate questions, lifestyle
Key words Birthday, different, names, same, special, Sikh,
Resources ◆ PS1 I am Special

UNIT 1
Myself

LESSON 1
Who am I?

Background

One of life's big questions is 'Who am I?' We spend much time trying to work out our place in the overall scheme of things. Names are often used to give us a sense of personal identity. Various faiths often have naming customs, birth ceremonies and ways of initiating the young.

Focus General/Sikhism

Starting points

Invite a group of children to come to the front. Ask in what ways they are different, for example, height, sex, etc. **W1** Focus on observable differences. Ask in what ways they are the same, for example, all have two eyes, etc.

Activities

Ask each child to complete photocopysheet 1 (PS1) 'I am Special' and use it as an opportunity to stress some ways in which each person is individual and special.

a) Before the children draw themselves, talk about eye and hair colour, shape of the face and facial features, etc.
b) Ask what children know about their names. Were they named after someone? Who? Why? Do they know the meaning of their names? Tell them of the Sikh custom for naming children. **W2**
c) The line beginning 'I am ...' could be used in any of the following ways.
   • Ages and birthdays. Why and how are these important?
   • Physical characteristics. What makes us look distinctive?
   • Personal Qualities. What sort of person am I? (For example, ... kind, ...thoughtful.)
d) Use the line beginning 'I can ...' to acknowledge some of the children's skills, aptitudes, abilities, and achievements they have made. For example, I can write or swim.
e) The last line could be used to record some of their attitudes and preferences. What sort of things do they like doing? What is their favourite food, song, book, etc?

Development

Make a class birthday graph. Which special people's birthdays do we celebrate? **W3** Ask if any of the children know anything of their faith's birth customs or ceremonies. **W4**

Watchpoints

W1 *Be sensitive to children with marked physical differences or disabilities.*

W2 *Male Sikhs take the last name 'Singh', meaning 'lion' and females have the last name 'Kaur', meaning 'princess' to show that everyone is equal. When a baby is taken to the gurdwara, the Sikh temple, for the first time, the Guru Granth Sahib is opened at random and the parents are given the first letter on the left-hand page. They must choose a name beginning with this letter for their baby.*

W3 *Christians celebrate the birth of Jesus.*

W4 *When a Sikh baby is first born a drop of honey is placed on his or her tongue to symbolise good and pure words. Immediately after birth the words of the Mul Mantra, the basic statement of Sikh belief, may be whispered in the baby's ear. 'There is one God, Eternal Truth is his name, maker of all and present in all.'*

Learning outcomes

◆ All should be able to describe some similarities to others and some differences.
◆ Some may be able to to list five ways in which they are special.
◆ A few may be able to explain why names are important and say something about Sikh names.

PS2

My Feelings Diary

	Draw or write about something that happened. Was anyone else involved?	How did you feel?
Monday		
Tuesday		
Wednesday		
Thursday		
Friday		

Key concept Ultimate questions, lifestyle

Key words Feelings (adjectives describing feelings, for example, happy, sad, etc.)

Resources ◆ PS2 My Feelings Diary ◆ PS31 (page 74)

UNIT 1

Myself

LESSON 2

How do I feel?

Background

A key tenet of many faiths is concerned with treating others in a way in which we would like to be treated. Learning about and understanding our own feelings and empathising with the feelings of others is an important part of being able to achieve this.

Focus General

Starting points

Initiate discussion of feelings by showing some simple outline pictures with different facial expressions, PS31. Ask children how they think these people feel. Why do they they think they feel like this? Ask some 'How do you feel when ...?' questions (for example, when you learn to swim? When you are lost?) Ask some 'What makes you feel...?' questions (consider a whole range of feelings here). Think how people express their feelings by facial expressions, body posture, and the way they behave. Consider how the way we act and behave affects the way others feel. How do we hurt others' feelings? **W1**

Activities

Use PS2 'My Feelings Diary'. Show the children how to keep the diary and set aside a short time each day for completing it. Keep the diary for a week. Encourage the children to try to record a different feeling each day if possible. At the end of the week reflect on the range of feelings children have experienced. Look in more depth at one or two feelings. Ask children to think of occasions when they felt like this. Who was involved? What happened? **W2**

Development

Read stories and reflect on how different characters feel. Look in a mirror. Make faces expressing different emotions. Think about what happens to our faces. Explore various feelings through music, mime and drama. Do animals have feelings? Think of other ways people express their feelings. For example, through letters, poetry, or cards. Write a letter or card to a friend or relative. Make a list of things you can do for others to make them feel happy.

Watchpoints

W1 *Ask the children to give examples of how being hurt physically and being hurt inside are different.*

W2 *Brainstorm words related to that feeling, for example, laughing, joy, smiling. Write a simple list poem about that feeling, beginning, for example, 'Happiness is …'. Paint pictures using colours which reflect that feeling, for example, red, yellow and orange for anger.*

Learning outcomes

◆ All should be able to name four different feelings they have.
◆ Some may be able to explain some of the ways in which people express their feelings.
◆ A few may be able to identify why a situation gave rise to a specific feeling, and describe how they felt.

A Celebration

What will you celebrate? _____

What will you wear?

Who will be there?

What will you eat?

What will you do?

Key concept Lifestyle, belonging, commitment

Key words Caring, celebration, family, home, Jewish, responsibility, Shabbat, sharing

Resources ◆ Poster 1 ◆ PS3 A Celebration

UNIT 1

Myself

LESSON 3

At Home

Background

Our homes are formative influences on our values, attitudes and belief systems. Shabbat is the Jewish day of rest, celebrating the creation of the world, as told in the Torah, and the rest God took on the seventh day. It begins at sunset on Friday evening and ends at sunset on Saturday. It is an occasion for the whole family to come together. The meal follows a set pattern and is full of symbolism and ritual. Great care is taken with the food and setting the table for the Shabbat meal. The family wash and put on their best clothes.

Focus Judaism

Starting points

Discuss with children what a home is for: shelter; somewhere to sleep; a place to eat; a place to keep things. What kind of things do we do at home? What things might families do together? (Shopping, picnicking, watching TV, eating, playing games, going on holiday.)

Activities

Look at and discuss the poster, stressing the importance of Shabbat in the routine of a typical Jewish family; giving security, a sense of identity and opportunities for families to get together. **W1**

Discuss and complete the PS3 'A Celebration'. Think of different family celebrations like birthdays, religious festivals, weddings. Choose one of these. Draw or write about the special things children do on these these occasions.

Ask children to think of different ways in which they are cared for and provided for in the home. What jobs are necessary in the home? How do jobs get done? How do the children help?

Development

What would it be like to be homeless? Discuss people who live nomadic lives. What are the problems for them? Emphasise the stability of a home, using the Jewish family as an example. **W2**

Watchpoints

W1 *On the table are two special loaves, covered with a cloth. The two plaited loaves remind Jews of God's gift of manna to their ancestors whilst travelling in the desert in exile. The cloth represents the dew which settled on the desert. There is also a cup of wine, some salt and some candles. The mother lights the candles and says a blessing to welcome the start of Shabbat. The father reads the scriptures and recalls the reason for Shabbat. He blesses and shares the wine and removes the white cloth and breaks the bread and shares that too, sprinkling it with salt.*

W2 *Historically the Jewish people have often lived nomadic lives or been dispersed. For example, the Israelites' wanderings in the desert.*

Learning outcomes

◆ All should be able to state some reasons why a home is important and know that Shabbat is a special day for Jewish people.
◆ Some may be able to describe in reasonable detail the Shabbat meal.
◆ A few may be able to offer more than one reason why Shabbat is important to a Jewish family.

STANLEY THORNES
infant RE

PS4

Family Portraits

This is ─────────────

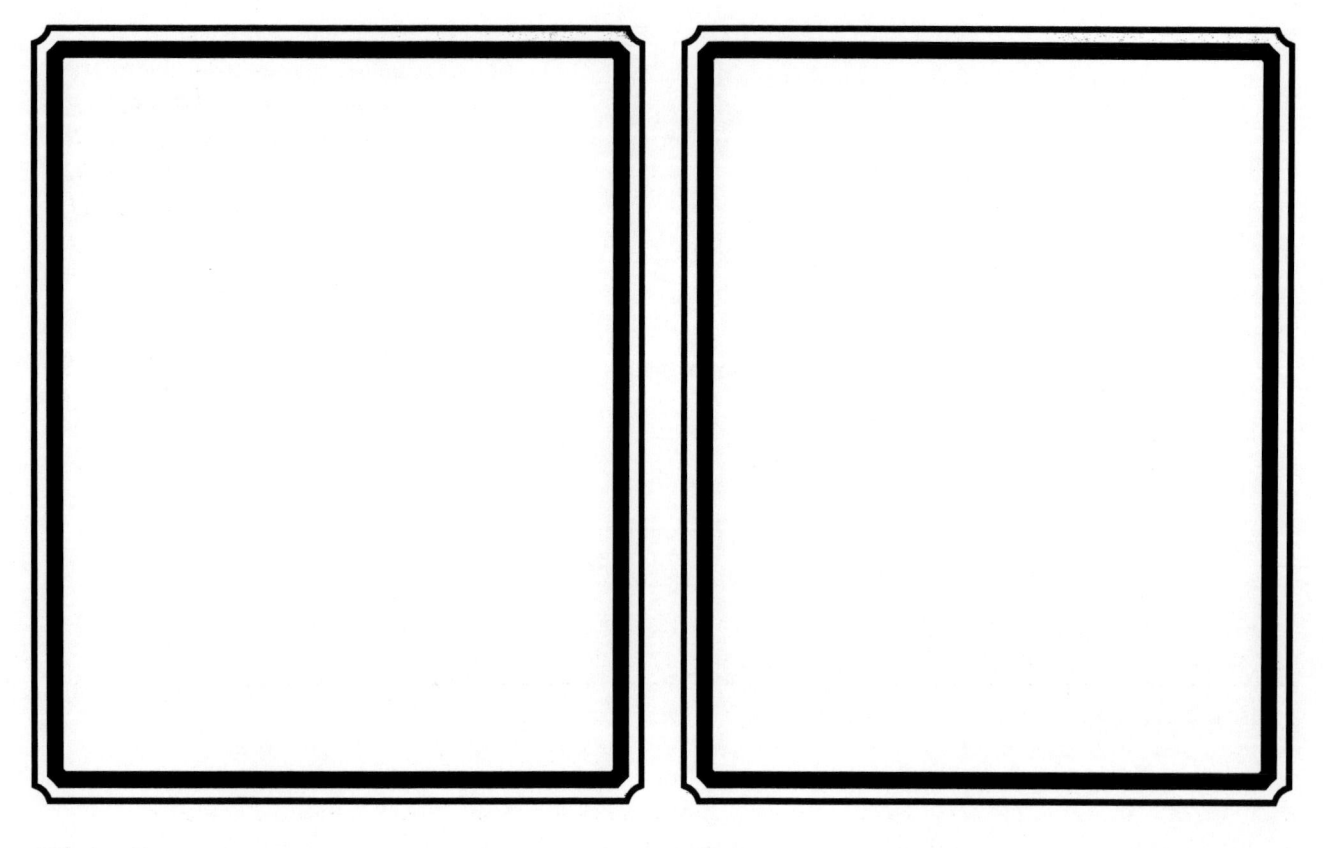

This is ───────── This is ─────────

Key concept Lifestyle, belonging, commitment

Key words Care, elders, family, Hindu, love, protect, rakhis, Raksha Bandhan, relations, respect

Resources ◆ Poster 2 ◆ PS4 Family Portraits ◆ String, wool, metal foil (for rakhis) ◆ Poem 'Our Family' (page 78)

UNIT 1

Myself

LESSON 4

My Family

Background

Family units may vary enormously in composition and culture. Hindu families place great importance on family relationships and show respect for the older members of the family. Many Hindus live in extended families.

Focus Hinduism

Starting points

Look at and discuss the poster. Talk about family size, age of members, and generations. Elicit children's views on what a family is. Ensure all children's ideas are treated as being equally valid. Discuss brother and sister relationships. In what ways do they look after one another? What do they share? Are they treated the same in all ways at all times? What do they do to show they care about members of their family? Discuss the Hindu idea of 'rakhis'. **W1**

Activities

Ask children to complete the PS4 'Family Portaits': one of their drawings should be a child, one a parent or adult carer and one another relative, preferably an older person such as a grandparent. Ask children to bring in photographs of their families for a class 'family' album. **W2** Discuss the ages of people in the family. Who is the eldest? Who is the youngest? What are the good and bad things about being young? Make and decorate some 'rakhis' with tinsel for a brother or write a thank-you card to a sister.

What are the good and bad things about being old? What can we learn from older generations? **W3**

Can people still be part of a family if they don't live in the same house? Ask children to name relatives who do not live with them. Think of ways of keeping in touch with them (visits, telephone, letters, photos, etc.). Locate where relatives live on a map. Discuss how some children have relatives in other countries, who might live in very different ways.

Watchpoints

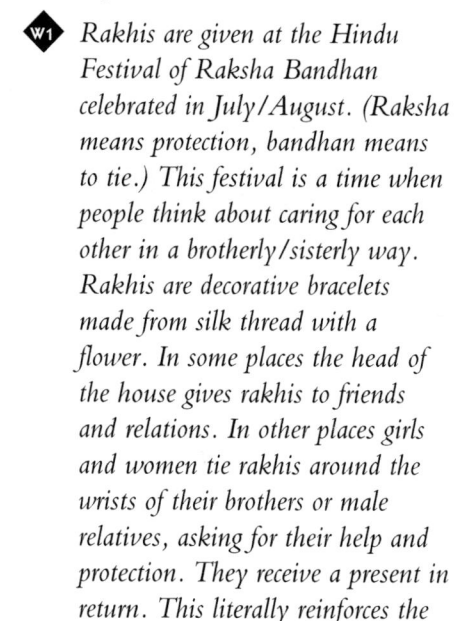

W1 *Rakhis are given at the Hindu Festival of Raksha Bandhan celebrated in July/August. (Raksha means protection, bandhan means to tie.) This festival is a time when people think about caring for each other in a brotherly/sisterly way. Rakhis are decorative bracelets made from silk thread with a flower. In some places the head of the house gives rakhis to friends and relations. In other places girls and women tie rakhis around the wrists of their brothers or male relatives, asking for their help and protection. They receive a present in return. This literally reinforces the idea of family ties, friendship and loyalty.*

W2 *Ensure all photos are labelled on the reverse. Be sensitive to children who do not have a 'family', or who are separated from their families.*

W3 *Hindus hold elders in great respect and learn from them.*

Development

Read the poem 'Our Family' (page 78). Consider the ways in which the class (or world) might be considered as a large family.

Learning outcomes

◆ All should be able to say why families are important and know that Raksha Bandhan is a Hindu festival.
◆ Some may be able to explain what 'rakhis' symbolise and know that Hindus respect their elders.
◆ A few should understand that family can be interpreted in a broader sense and explain this.

My Day

In the morning I _____
_____
_____

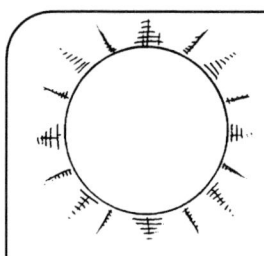

In the afternoon I _____
_____
_____

In the evening I _____
_____
_____

In the night I _____
_____
_____

Key concept Lifestyle, beliefs and values, commitment

Key words Adhan, day, night, prayer, sunrise, sunset

Resources ◆ Poster 3 ◆ PS5 My Day ◆ PS32 Enlarged picture Muslim prayer timetable (page 75) ◆ Local newspaper, magazines with pictures of day and night

UNIT 1

Myself

LESSON 5

My Day

Background

All our lives are governed by routines to some extent. Routines are particularly important in establishing order and security. Prayer (salah) is part of a Muslim's daily life. Salah is the second of the Five Pillars (fundamentals) of Islam. Most Muslims pray five times a day, wherever they are, at prescribed times. These are: Fajr (morning, between dawn and sunrise); Zuhr (midday or early afternoon); Asr (late afternoon); Maghrib (evening, around sunset); Isha (night, before going to bed). These times change with the times of sunset and sunrise. Mosques usually provide lists of current prayer times.

Focus Islam

Starting points

Look at the poster. Ask children to describe what is happening in each picture, and to sort them into chronological order. Ask them to think of other things they do every day (for example, cleaning teeth, taking pets for a walk, tidying up). Clock faces could be completed, showing the times at which these occur. **W1** Try to sort the events into order of importance. Help children find night and day pictures. Make a night and day collage.

Activities

Ask the children to complete PS5 'My Day' by selecting one important thing they do at each of the times shown. Explain simply how prayer plays an important part in Muslim life. **W2**

Make a large version of the Muslim prayer timetable PS32. There are no times on the clock. Do children know what sunrise and sunset mean? Help them to use local newspapers to find times of sunrise and sunset for different days. **W3**

Development

Do the children sometimes forget to do important things? How do they feel at these times? How do people remind themselves to do important things? (Leave notes, use a calendar or diary, etc.) Think of some important events coming up and make some sort of reminders. How do Muslims remember when to pray? **W4**

Watchpoints

W1 *Some children may know of people who sleep at day and work at night.*

W2 *Some children say prayers at home and have included this on their sheets.*

W3 *The amount of daylight lengthens/shortens according to the time of year.*

W4 *Muslims may keep notes of the times in prominent places, or, if they live near enough to a mosque, hear the adhan, the call to prayer.*

Learning outcomes

◆ All should be able to describe some important things they do each day and say that Muslims pray at special times every day.
◆ Some may be able to describe prayers, referring to the times of sunrise and sunset.
◆ A few may be able to give the names of the prayer times.

WANTED

A Good Friend

I am looking for someone who is

_____

How could you be a good friend?

_____

Key concept Lifestyle, commitment

Key words Friends, Naomi, Ruth, words related to the qualities of friendship (for example, kind, loyal)

Resources ◆ PS6 Wanted ◆ Story of Ruth and Naomi (page 95)

UNIT 1

Myself

LESSON 6

My Friends

Background

Consideration for others is a concept enshrined in the belief systems of many religions. The story of Ruth and Naomi is used to bring out important aspects of relationships. For children, making friends is often the first step outside the family circle towards a wider social awareness.

Focus Christianity/Judaism

Starting points

Read and discuss the story of Ruth and Naomi (page 95). Ask children what they would feel like if they moved to a new school. How can they make newcomers feel welcomed?

Activities

Ask the children what they like about their friends. (For example, they are good fun, they share their toys, they are kind.) What sort of things do they prefer to do on their own? What sort of things do they like to do with friends? Complete PS6 'Wanted poster'. Encourage the children to draw a good friend as a model and use some of ideas and words already discussed.

Development

Ask the children if they know of any other stories from religious books about friends. **W1** Celebrate friendship and have a Friendship Day or Week. Have a friendship service in which everyone lights a candle and in the quietness of their own minds says thank-you for a particular friend. Write a card saying something nice to someone who isn't a friend. Write a class list poem with each line beginning, A friend is someone who ... **W2**

Look at the hands on a 50p coin symbolising the hand of friendship. **W3**

Ask children to draw round the outline of their hands and decorate them (or simply use handprints) to encircle the classroom, symbolising the joined hands of friendship. List as many words as possible which mean 'friend'. Discuss the idea that you do not have to live near someone to be their friend, for example, pen friends.

Watchpoints

W1 *The story of David and Jonathan is another example (1 Samuel 17–24)*

W2 *Children could make a friendship cake as a class and serve each other a slice, suggest the words of a toast, and toast each other with fruit juice.*

W3 *The Olympic rings also symbolise unity and friendship.*

Learning outcomes

◆ All should be able to state some things friends do together.
◆ Some may be able to re-tell the story of Ruth and Naomi and state some qualities of friendship.
◆ A few may be able to identify and name several positive characteristics of Ruth's character.

Jesus' Friends

Andrew	Peter	James
Matthew	Thomas	Simon
Judas	Bartholomew	Philip
James	Thaddeus	John

Key concept Authority, inspiration, belonging, commitment

Key words Disciples (followers), fishermen, Jesus, the names of some disciples, Zaccheus

Resources ◆ PS7 Jesus' Friends ◆ Story: Jesus Meets the Disciples (page 87) ◆ Story: Zaccheus (page 97) ◆ Story: Peter Denies Jesus (page 93)

UNIT 1

Myself

LESSON 7

Jesus' Friends

Background

The Bible says that when Jesus was about thirty years old, he began to travel around the country, preaching and healing. Many people followed him. Jesus chose some special friends called disciples (learners) to help him. They stayed with him all the time and gave up their jobs. They were ordinary men. They were not rich, important or clever, but they had one thing in common - they loved God. At least seven of his disciples were fishermen.

Focus Christianity

Starting points

Ask the children what they look for when they choose a friend. How do you know when someone wants to be your friend? What do they do? How do you respond?

Ask children what sort of things they quarrel about with friends. How do they make up? Why is it good to have some special friends? Give the children a little background about Jesus and his disciples.

Activities

Read and discuss the story of Jesus meeting his disciples (page 87). Use PS7 'Jesus' Friends'. Ask how many 'special' friends Jesus had. Which two were twins? Did any have the same names? **W1**

Talk about how Jesus befriended some rather unlikely characters, whom others thought of in disdain. The story of Zaccheus (page 97) is a good example of this. **W2**

Development

Ask the children if they have ever been left out of others' games or excluded in some way because they were different from the others. How did they feel? Ask some 'what if ...' questions posing some moral dilemmas. For example, do you always do what your friend is doing? What if they call someone else names? What if you see them stealing? What would you do? Ask the children if they have ever been let down by their friends. Read the story of Peter denying Jesus (page 93). **W3**

Watchpoints

W1 *The pictures may be stuck onto card, cut out and arranged alphabetically; two sets could be combined and pairs of children play snap or pelmanism with them; the pictures could be stuck on lollipop sticks and used like puppets to act out stories from the Bible involving the disciples.*

W2 *Zaccheus was an outsider because he was a tax collector. He was working for the Romans and made his own living out of the taxes he collected. He was not a popular man.*

W3 *Even some of Jesus' best friends let him down at times.*

Learning outcomes

◆ All should know that Jesus had a close group of friends, and name at least two of them.
◆ Some should know that Jesus chose his friends specifically to help him in his ministry.
◆ A few may be able to re-tell the story of Zaccheus or of Peter denying Jesus and be able to explain what is significant about the story.

How I Can Help

☆ Draw pictures to show how you can help others.
☆ Write about the pictures.

I can help ——————
——————————
——————————
——————————
——————————

I can help ——————
——————————
——————————
——————————
——————————

I can help ——————
——————————
——————————
——————————
——————————

Key concept Lifestyle, commitment, beliefs and values

Key words Community, helping, langar, Muslim, sharing, Sikh, zakah,

Resources
◆ PS8 How I Can Help   ◆ Story 'What it's worth' (page 97)

UNIT 1

Myself

LESSON 8

Thinking of Others

Background

Zakah is one of the Five Pillars (fundamentals) of Islam. It involves the regular giving of a proportion of one's money to support other Muslims and people in need. Every Sikh temple (gurdwara) has a langar (dining room). Sikhs believe in providing food for all who come into the temple regardless of whether they are Sikhs or not.

Focus Islam/Sikhism

Starting points

Read and discuss the 'What it's worth' story (page 97). **W1**

What we say and do affects others. Invite children to ask for something in different ways (for example, quietly, rudely, angrily, sadly, happily). Ask if it affects the way we respond. Ask the children to think of something nice to say to each other. How does it make them feel? What sort of things do people say that are hurtful? Ask the children when it is acceptable and unacceptable to do these: shout, run, throw things, push, etc. **W2**

Activities

Discuss the school as a community and the need for people to work together. List the people who help in school. Question them about their jobs. How can we make our school a better place?

Show how thinking of others is demonstrated by Sikhs through the provision of the 'langar'. **W3** Discuss and complete the PS8 'How I Can Help'. This can be used in connection with the home, the classroom, the school, the wider community or in relation to particular groups, for example, the elderly, younger children, etc.

Development

List people who help us in our community. Consider the difficulties of specific people in our community, for example, the disabled. What difficulties might they experience? What help is provided? Are there any practical ways we can help?

Watchpoints

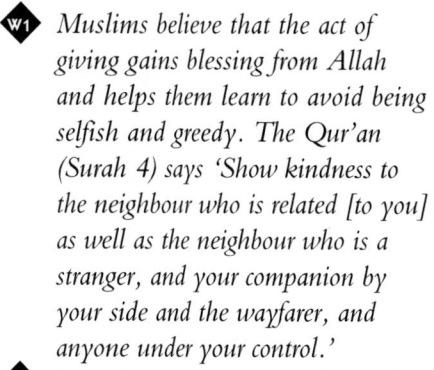

W1 *Muslims believe that the act of giving gains blessing from Allah and helps them learn to avoid being selfish and greedy. The Qur'an (Surah 4) says 'Show kindness to the neighbour who is related [to you] as well as the neighbour who is a stranger, and your companion by your side and the wayfarer, and anyone under your control.'*

W2 *Knowing when you can do certain things is important.*

W3 *All members of the Sikh community, including children, are expected to help in the langar. Eating together and serving each other is seen as part of worship. This is an expression of 'sewa' or service. Guru Granth Sahib 4 states 'There can be no worship without performing good deeds.'*

Learning outcomes

◆ All should see the importance of thinking of others and name some people who help in school.
◆ Some should know about some of the ways in which Muslims or Sikhs believe in helping others.
◆ A few may be able to explain 'zakah' or what a 'langar' is.

STANLEY THORNES
infant RE

PS9

Making a Badge

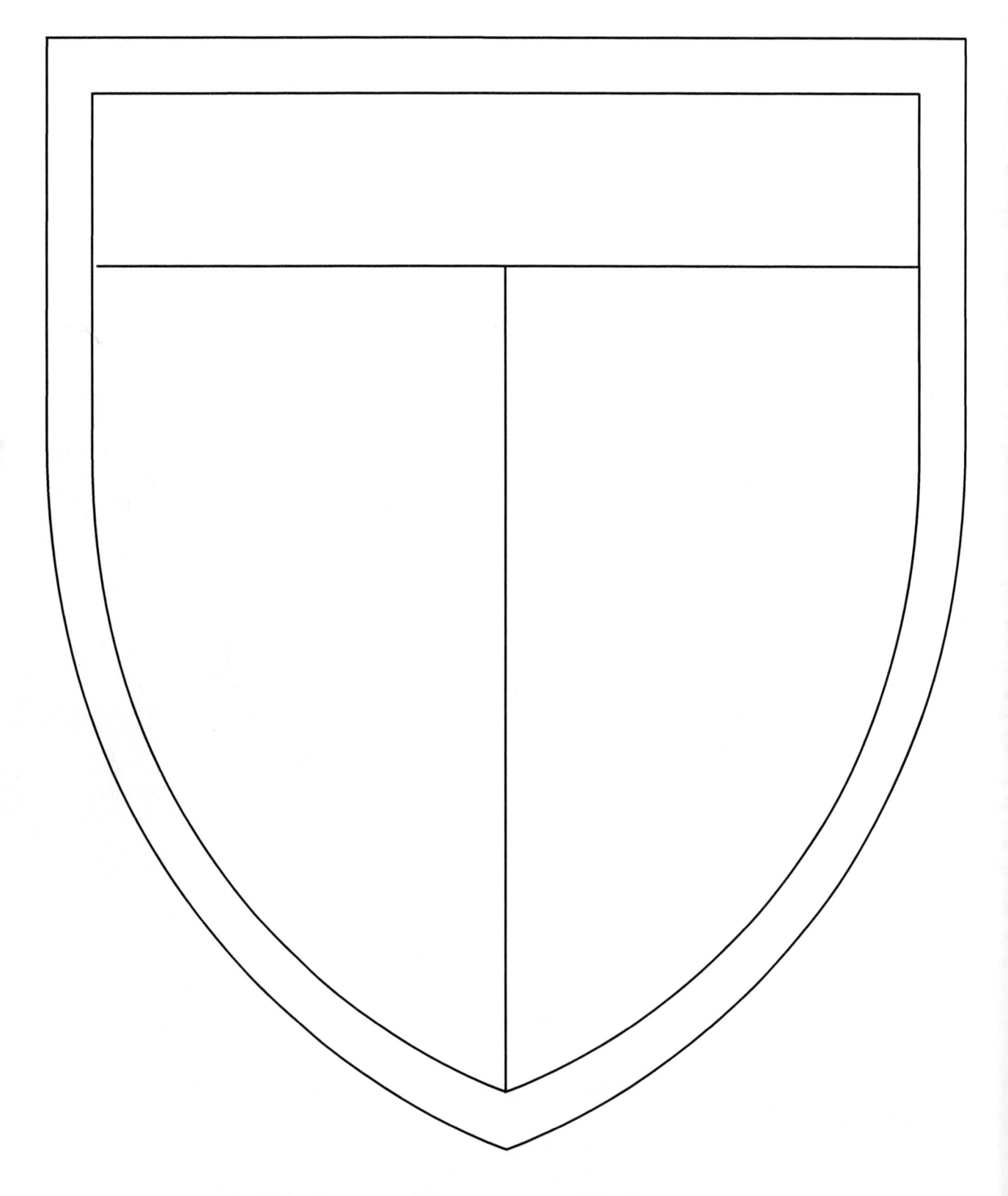

- ◆ Write the name of the group at top of the badge.
- ◆ Draw where the group lives or meets in the space on the left.
- ◆ Draw something special about the group on the right.

Key concept Lifestyle, symbolism, belonging

Key words belong, clothes, group, the Five Ks (Kachera, Kara, Kirpan, Kesh, Kangha), Sikh

Resources ◆ Poster 4 ◆ PS9 Making a Badge

UNIT 1

Myself

LESSON 9

Belonging

Background

We all belong to a variety of different groups, for example, family, school, faith community. Clothes are sometimes worn as a symbol of belonging to a particular group.

Focus Sikhism

Starting points

Look at the poster. Explain who the boy is, and what various aspects of his dress and the things he is holding signify. **W1** Bring out the point that his dress is a symbol of belonging to a particular group. Discuss his hair. How is it kept tidy? Also note that younger boys don't wear turbans. **W2**

Ask children to name other people who wear special clothes, which mark them out as belonging to a particular group (for example, police, etc.). Does your school have a uniform or badge? How do the children feel when they wear it? What difference does it make to them when they wear a school uniform or badge?

Activities

Ask the children which groups they belong to and list them (for example, family, faith groups). Which did they choose to belong to? Draw some of the activities they do with these groups. Make a display. Make a chart to show some of the advantages and disadvantages of belonging to some of the groups. **W3**

Being a member of a group has certain responsibilities and duties. Ask the children to think of some of these in relation to the family or another group. How can people recognize that you belong to particular groups? (Name, uniform, etc.) Use PS9 'Making a Badge' and get children to make up a badge for a group they belong to, for example, family or class. **W4**

Development

Why do we have family names? Talk about the meaning of some family names.

Investigate faith group symbols.

Watchpoints

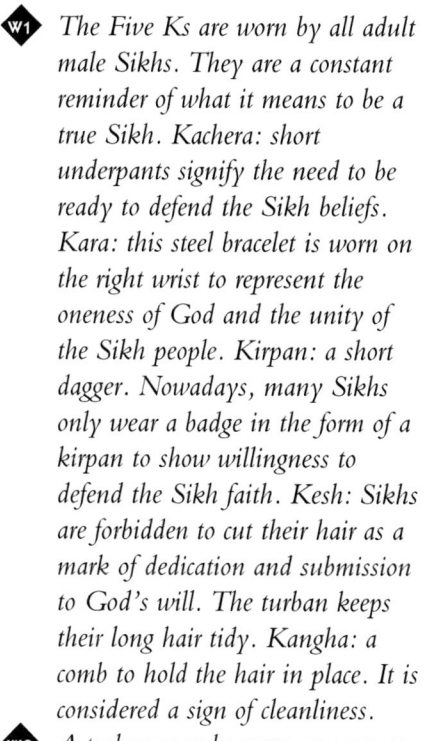

W1 *The Five Ks are worn by all adult male Sikhs. They are a constant reminder of what it means to be a true Sikh. Kachera: short underpants signify the need to be ready to defend the Sikh beliefs. Kara: this steel bracelet is worn on the right wrist to represent the oneness of God and the unity of the Sikh people. Kirpan: a short dagger. Nowadays, many Sikhs only wear a badge in the form of a kirpan to show willingness to defend the Sikh faith. Kesh: Sikhs are forbidden to cut their hair as a mark of dedication and submission to God's will. The turban keeps their long hair tidy. Kangha: a comb to hold the hair in place. It is considered a sign of cleanliness.*

W2 *A turban may be worn as soon as a boy is able to tie it for himself.*

W3 *For example, the family: advantages – provides love, care, food, shelter; disadvantages – arguments, jobs you have to do.*

W4 *Something special about the group to draw could be a person, activity, group, pet, etc.*

Learning outcomes

◆ All should be able to name and describe some of the groups they belong to.

◆ Some may be able to describe the way an adult male Sikh dresses and name other groups which might be identified by the way they dress.

◆ A few may be able to name some of the symbols used by different faith groups.

A Special Baby

☆ Colour the pictures. ☆ Cut them out. ☆ Put them in order.

Key concept Authority, inspiration, beliefs, values

Key words Baby, Bethlehem, celebrate, Christians, Jesus, Joseph, Mary, shepherds, stable, star, wise men

Resources ◆ PS10 A Special Baby ◆ Christmas Story (pages 81–83) ◆ Christina Rossetti poem (page 80) ◆ Mothercare catalogue

UNIT 1

Myself

LESSON 10

A Special Baby
(The Christmas Story)

Background

Christmas is the Christian festival celebrating the birth of Christ. Christians believe that Jesus is the Son of God, was born of the Virgin Mary, and had no human father.

Focus Christianity

Starting points

Encourage children to tell anecdotes about their experiences of babies. Ask children to list some of the preparations that must take place before the birth of a baby. **W1** What sort of things happen immediately after the birth? (Visitors, cards, gifts, flowers.) Make a 'Congratulations' card. Look in retailers' catalogues for baby gifts and things a baby needs.

Activities

Ask children to talk about their expectations of Christmas. Talk about giving rather than receiving, how they prepare, how they feel. Ask why Christmas is a very special time for Christians. **W2**

Tell the Christmas story in your own words. If possible, tell it in three short sessions. Discuss each section.

Ask children to complete PS10 'A Special Baby'. Cut out the pictures and re-order them to tell the Christmas story. Write a caption under each picture. Encourage the children to use their pictures to re-tell the story to a partner in their own words.

Development

Re-tell the story from different points of view. (For example, the shepherds or the inn-keeper.) Use the pictures from PS10 'A Special Baby' as the basis for making a six-picture advent calendar or Christmas cards. **W3**

Ask children to think about 'precious things'. What things can they think of which are of special significance to them? Does 'expensive' mean 'most valuable'? Can an action sometimes be better than a gift? Read the Christina Rossetti poem (page 80).

Watchpoints

W1 *For example, getting a cot, getting baby clothes and nappies, decorating the room, toys, thinking of names.*

W2 *For Christians Christmas is a time for celebrating the birth of a very special baby – Jesus Christ whom they believe was God's special gift to the world. They believe that Jesus sacrificed his life for them, and through him they can be forgiven for their sins and come to know God in a personal way. To them Jesus provides an 'ideal' model for living.*

W3 *Advent literally means 'the coming'.*

Learning outcomes

◆ All should be able to give reasons why a baby is special and know that Christmas is the Christian festival celebrating the birth of Jesus.

◆ Some may be able to re-tell the Christmas story in reasonable detail.

◆ A few may be able to explain why Jesus is very special to Christians.

STANLEY THORNES
infant RE

UNIT 2

New Life

INTRODUCTION

This unit is designed to help children reflect on, and respond to, the wonder of the world around them. It will help raise their awareness of its cyclical and patterned nature. Throughout the unit, questions of meaning and purpose will be explored. Children will be encouraged to appreciate their role in respecting and caring for the world and all living things.

Unit 2 – Overview

Lesson	Contents	Key Concepts	Religious Focus
1	**The Creation** People have always discussed where they came from and how life began. Most religions offer some form of explanation. ♦ How did the world begin? ♦ Is there a creator God? ♦ How do Christianity and Judaism explain this?	Ultimate questions, beliefs, values	Christianity/ Judaism
2	**Caring for the Environment** The idea that humans have a custodial responsibility for taking care of the world is common to many faiths. ♦ Who 'owns' the world? ♦ What is our responsibility? ♦ What can we learn from Noah?	Lifestyle, beliefs, values	Christianity/ Judaism/Islam
3	**Hurt no Living Thing** The first Buddhist precept states; 'Be sympathetic and helpful to all things that have life and be careful not to harm or kill any living creature.' ♦ How are animals and humans similar? ♦ What is our responsibility towards animals? ♦ What do Buddhists believe?	Lifestyle, beliefs, values	Buddhism
4	**The Seasons** Our lives are influenced by regular natural cycles such as the seasons. ♦ What are the four seasons? ♦ What are their characteristics? ♦ Which religious festivals are linked to the seasons?	Lifestyle, symbolism	General

Lesson	Contents	Key Concepts	Religious Focus
5	**Life Cycles** In nature there are clearly discernible life cycles. ♦ What stages do we pass through in our life? ♦ What do Buddhists believe about life? ♦ What do Christians believe about death?	Ultimate questions beliefs, values	Christianity/ Buddhism
6	**Growing Things** We all marvel at the potential of tiny seeds to grow into large plants. A sense of awe and wonder is promoted by growing and observing things. ♦ Who put the potential to grow into tiny seeds? ♦ Who was Johnny Appleseed? ♦ Who made us?	Ultimate questions, symbolism	General
7	**Babies** There is something wonderful and beautiful about new babies. Most faiths have their own birth ceremonies and customs. ♦ What happens at the baptism of a Christian baby? ♦ What symbolism is involved in the ceremony? ♦ What birth customs are associated with Hinduism?	Belonging, commitment, symbolism	Christianity/ Hinduism
8	**Holi** Holi is a Hindu Spring festival. ♦ What is the story behind Holi? ♦ How do people celebrate Holi? ♦ What symbolism is associated with the festival?	Belonging, symbolism	Hinduism
9	**The Story of Easter** Easter is one of the most significant Christian festivals. It is a time of both sadness and rejoicing for Christians. ♦ What happened at the first Easter? ♦ How can it be both happy and sad? ♦ What does Easter mean to Christians?	Authority, inspiration, beliefs, values, commitment	Christianity
10	**Easter Customs and Symbols** There are many different customs and traditions associated with the celebration of Easter which often have deeper symbolic meaning. ♦ What do children think of at Easter? ♦ How do people celebrate Easter? ♦ What is the meaning behind some Easter symbols?	Symbolism, belonging	Christianity

The Creation

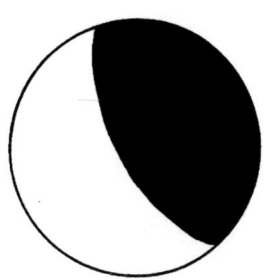

Day ☐

God made the sun, moon and stars.

Day ☐

God made light and dark

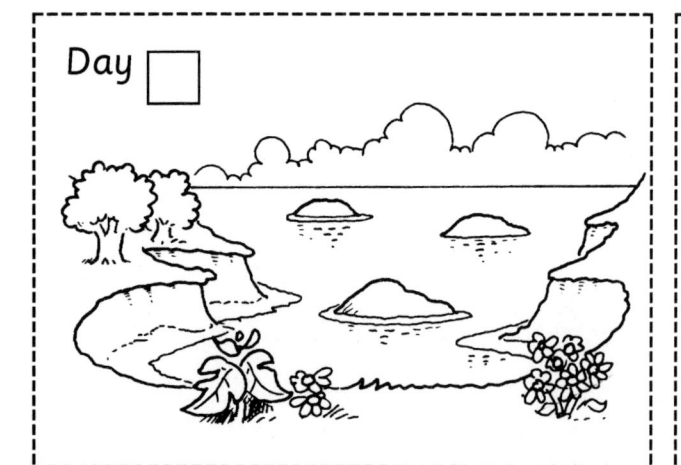

Day ☐

God made the birds and the fish.

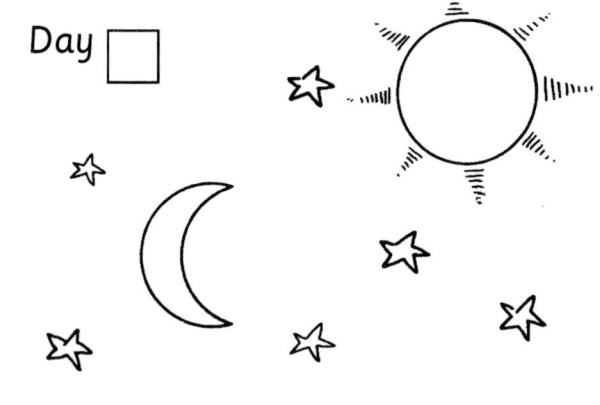

Day ☐

God made the animals and human beings.

Day ☐

God made the sky.

Day ☐

God made the earth, with plants and trees. God made the sea.

Key concept Ultimate questions, beliefs and values

Key words Creation, Christians, God, Jews, manufactured, natural

Resources
- PS11 The Creation
- 'Who put the colours in the rainbow?' (page 80)
- The Creation Story (page 83)

UNIT 2

New Life

LESSON 1

The Creation

Background

For thousands of years people have been discussing where they came from and how the world began. Different religions often have different explanations. Christians and Jews share the same Creation story.

Focus Christianity/Judaism

Starting points

Take the children for a walk round the school field or local park. Ask them to look for things that are not manufactured, for example: the sun, sky, clouds, grass, trees, animals, insects. They should also look for things which are manufactured. Make two lists. Ask children to suggest where these things came from, how they were made or who made them. Focus on the theme 'what a wonderful world we live in'. **W1** Look at the words of 'Who put the colours in the rainbow?' (page 80). Discuss their meaning. Sing the song.

Activities

Tell the Creation story which is to be found in the Christian Bible and Jewish Torah (page 83). Ask children to cut out the words and pictures on PS11 'The Creation' and re-sequence them in the correct order. **W2** Write some thank you prayers for the wonder of our created world. **W3**

Development

Ask children how they feel when they have just mastered something difficult or made something that has required a lot of effort. Ask the children to consider what they might, or might not, have done if they had made the world. There are many opportunities for art links, for example, a large frieze or collage showing the events in the Creation story; silhouette skylines of trees, houses at day/night; positive/negative images/shapes emphasising light and dark; star or moon prints; themed 'what a wonderful world' pictures (plants, animals, fish, etc.). Make up some alphabetical lists, for example, think of an animal/fish/bird/tree for each letter of the alphabet. Find and read some other creation stories. **W4**

Watchpoints

W1 *If possible, play the Louis Armstrong song 'What a Wonderful World'.*

W2 *Stick these on to a long strip and make into mini-friezes or concertina books. Get children to retell the story in their own words, using their pictures.*

W3 *Christians and Jews believe Creation is a gift from God.*

W4 *Most faiths have a creation story in their scriptures. Explain that for thousands of years people have been discussing where they came from and how the world began.*

Learning outcomes

- All should be able to name several natural things and know that the Creation story from the Bible/Torah tells how Christians/Jews believe God made the world.
- Some may be able to recount the Creation Story from the Bible in accurate sequential detail.
- A few may be able to explain the significance of the rest day on the seventh day for God and people.

Spot the Litter

☆ Colour in all the litter you can find.

☆ Colour the cans red. ☆ Colour the crisp packets blue.

☆ Colour the paper green. ☆ Colour the bottles yellow.

I can find:

☐ cans ☐ crisp packets ☐ pieces of paper ☐ bottles

Key concept Values, beliefs, lifestyle

Key words Ark, care, environment, flood, khilafah, manufactured, natural, Noah, responsibility

Resources ◆ PS12 Spot the Litter ◆ Words to 'Think of a World Without Any Flowers' (page 79) ◆ Noah and the Ark (page 92)

UNIT 2

New Life

LESSON 2

Caring for the Environment

Background

The idea that humans have a custodial responsibility for taking care of the world is common to many faiths. Christians, Jews and Muslims believe that God made the Earth and all that is in it, and that people have been given the responsibility to care for it.

Focus Christianity/Judaism/Islam

Starting points

Read or sing 'Think of a world without any flowers' (page 79). What would life be like without all the things mentioned? Collect pictures (or use suitable videos) of natural things - fruit, flowers, sky with sun and clouds, etc. Ask the children: Who owns these natural things? Who has the right to use them? Who is responsible for looking after them. Give them the opportunity to choose each time from the following: everybody, the people who grow them, God or no one. **W1**

Activities

Ask children to name some natural disasters. What happens at these times? Read and discuss the story of Noah's Ark (page 92). What can we learn from the story about our responsibility for looking after the world? **W2**

Use the PS12 'Spot the Litter' sheet. **W3** Make a simple block graph showing the number of each of the items of rubbish found. Carry out your own school litter survey. Make 'Keep our School Clean' posters. Consider ways of improving the school environment.

Development

Discuss ways in which local authorities are helping to care for the environment. **W4**

Brainstorm ideas for ways in which we could care for the wider environment (for example, recycle cans; have fewer cars, etc.). Try recycling paper. **W5** Use the recycled 'pages' for writing slogans about care for the environment. **W6**

Watchpoints

W1 *The Islamic idea of stewardship is called khilafah. The Qur'an contains several references to people as trustees of the Earth, for example, 'It is He who has made you His agents, inheritors of the Earth.'*

W2 *The story of Noah is common to Christianity, Judaism and Islam.*

W3 *There are 10 cans, 8 crisp packets, 6 pieces of paper, 5 bottles.*

W4 *Many local authorities provide bottle, clothes, paper and metal banks, and make provision for sorting and recycling our rubbish.*

W5 *Collect a bucket of paper. Tear it into small pieces. Soak thoroughly. Squeeze excess water out. Lay paper pulp on a dry cloth. Squash it flat and fairly thin into small page-size pieces. Leave to dry.*

W6 *There are many ways in which nature recycles things around us, for example, plant waste into compost, the rain cycle.*

Learning outcomes

◆ All should be able to retell the story of Noah and the Ark in outline and should know that it is a story from the Christian, Jewish and Islamic faiths.
◆ Some may be able to explain the religious beliefs which lie behind the story of Noah's Ark and offer practical suggestions of ways in which individuals can help protect and care for the environment.
◆ A few may be able to explain the Muslim idea of 'khilafah'.

Pet's Page

What goes with each pet?

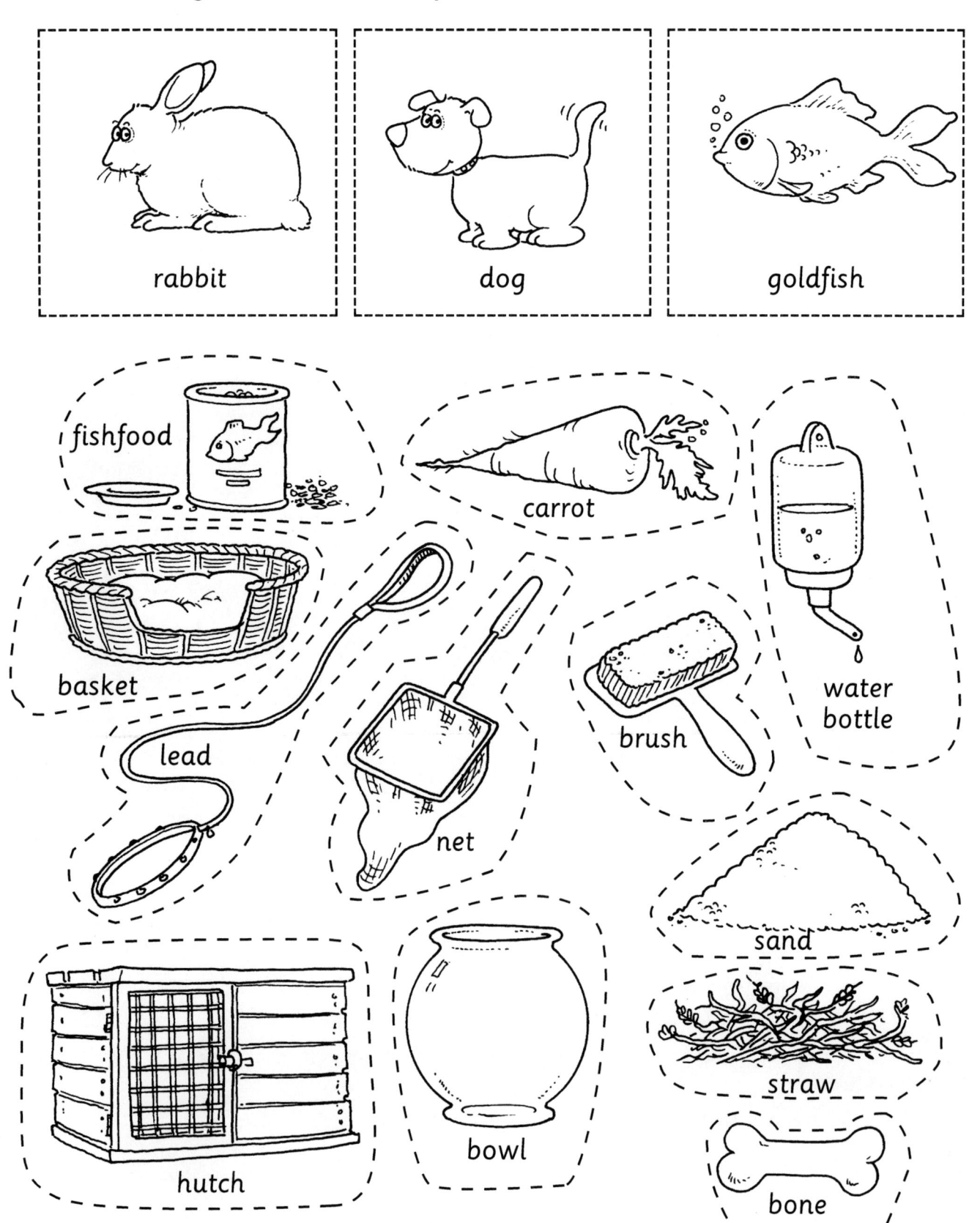

rabbit

dog

goldfish

fishfood

carrot

basket

lead

net

brush

water bottle

sand

hutch

bowl

straw

bone

Key concept Beliefs, values, lifestyle

Key words Animals, Buddha, Buddhist, care, insects, pets, responsibility

Resources ◆ Poster 5 ◆ PS13 Pet's Page ◆ Buddhist Prayer (page 78) ◆ Story 'The Swan' (page 95)

UNIT 2

New Life

LESSON 3

Hurt No Living Thing

Background

The founder of the Buddhist faith, the Buddha, laid down five rules for everyday life, called the Five Precepts. The first precept is as follows: 'Be sympathetic and helpful to all things that have life and be careful not to harm or kill any living creature.'

Focus Buddhism

Starting points

Look at the poster. Read the poem. Ask children what they know about each insect. Ask children if there are any insects they are afraid of. Talk about their fears. Ask children in what ways various insects are helpful. Stress the interdependence of living things. **W1** Ask children which animals help us and how. **W2**

Do animals have feelings or thoughts? Can they talk or communicate to each other or us? Relate these ideas to particular animals, for example, a dog, a bee. Consider the similarities and differences between humans and animals. In what way are some people unkind to animals? What can we do about this? **W3**

Activities

Look at PS13 'Pet's Page' together. Ensure all children know what each item is. Cut them out and sort them into groups with the appropriate pet. Use this activity as a means of talking about pets' physical needs like food, water, housing, exercise and grooming. Discuss why people keep pets. Stress that having a pet brings with it certain responsibilities. Read the story of 'The Swan' (page 95). What can we learn from this about attitudes to animals? **W4**

Development

Arrange a Day of Celebration for Pets. Arrange a Class Pet's Day, when children bring in photos of their pets and talk about them. Find out about the work of caring organisations like the RSPCA and PDSA. Read the Buddhist Prayer (page 78).

Watchpoints

W1 *Worms aerate the ground; bees provide honey; spiders keep down flies.*

W2 *Horses, some working dogs, bullocks and camels all help people.*

W3 *Buddhists believe that we should strive to be free from suffering and that we should not kill or cause injury.*

W4 *The story underlines Buddhist belief about the sanctity of all living creatures.*

Learning outcomes

◆ All should know that all animals perform different functions (jobs) and provide examples of two of these. They should be able to retell the story of 'The Swan' in reasonable detail.
◆ Some may be able to explain how to care for and look after one type of pet and know that Buddhists believe in the sanctity of all living creation.
◆ A few may be able to appreciate the interdependence of all forms of life and be able to offer an explanation as to why they think Buddhists believe no living thing should be harmed.

The Four Seasons

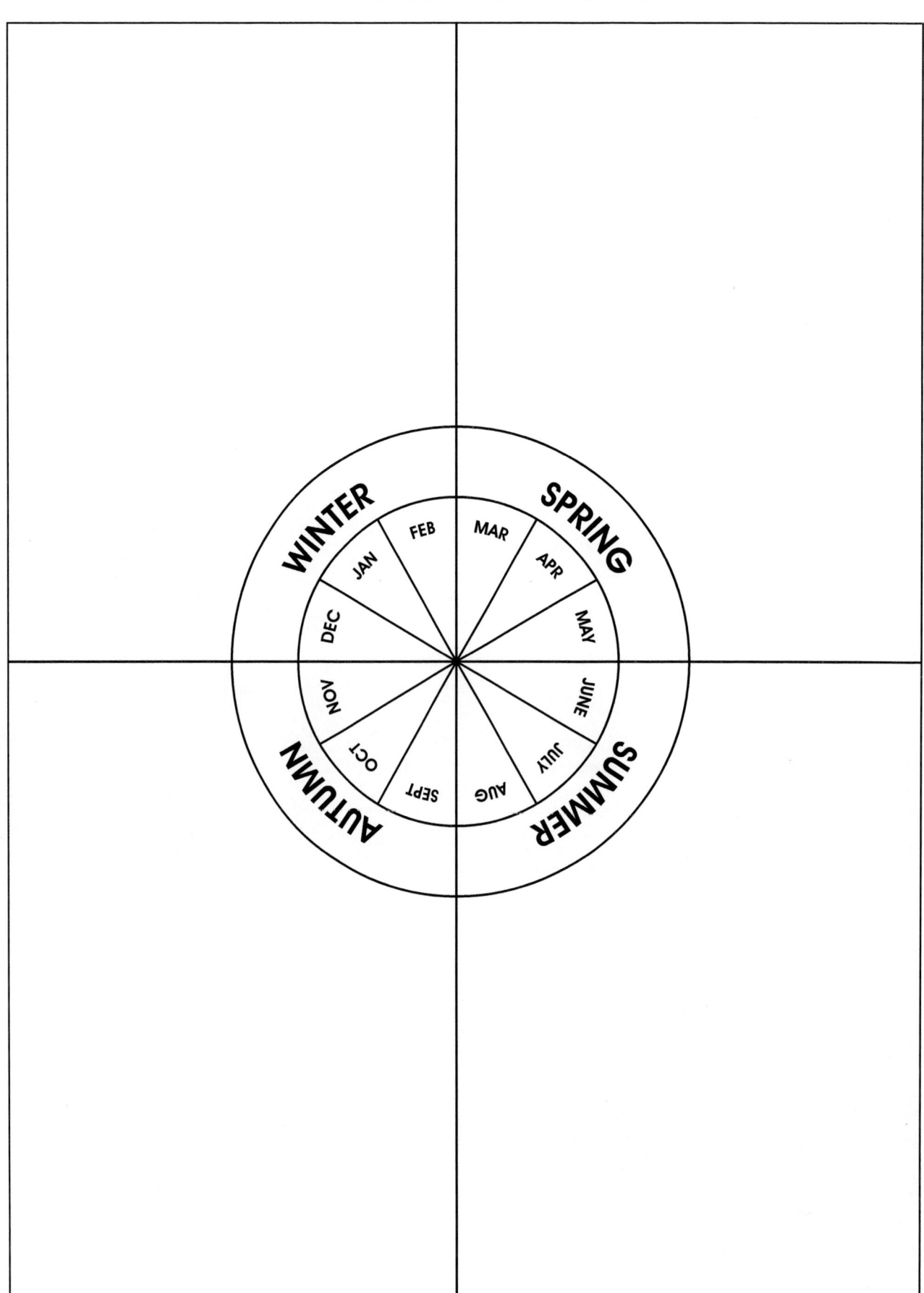

WINTER · SPRING · SUMMER · AUTUMN

JAN · FEB · MAR · APR · MAY · JUNE · JULY · AUG · SEPT · OCT · NOV · DEC

Key concept Symbolism, lifestyle

Key words Change, day (and names of days), festivals, month, seasons (and names of seasons), weather, week,

Resources
- ◆ Poster 6 ◆ PS14 The Four Seasons
- ◆ 'The Sun Wakes Up' (page 79)
- ◆ Religious Festivals Chart (page 102)
- ◆ 'Weather' poem (page 79)

UNIT 2

New Life

LESSON 4

The Seasons

Background

Our lives are governed by regular natural cycles: daily, monthly and seasonal, each with a range of different characteristics. Many religious festivals are related to the seasons.

Focus General

Starting points

Read the poem 'The Sun Wakes Up' (page 79) together. ◆W1◆ Discuss how each day has a regular pattern of changes. What sort of things do children do regularly at different times of day? Ask the children to list regular recurring schoolday routines. ◆W2◆ Name animals which only come out at night.

Ask children to sequence the days of the week. ◆W3◆

Play and discuss excerpts from Vivaldi's 'Four Seasons'

Activities

Look at the poster. Ask children to describe each picture and identify the similarities and differences in each picture. Ask them to talk about how each picture gradually changes. Ask children to name the four seasons and decide which picture represents each season. Mention different seasonal chracteristics. ◆W4◆

Ask children which season it is now. Go for a walk and look for seasonal signs. ◆W5◆ Use PS14 'The Four Seasons'. Ask children to draw something they associate with each season.

Development

Use an enlargement of the centre circle of PS14 for a display, with drawings and written work spread around it in appropriate places. It could be used to record birthdays, anniversaries, school events, seasonal pictures of the countryside and animal life, activities (picnics, snowballing), games, clothes, colours or weather associated with different seasons. Use it as a Festivals' Calendar. Add pictures and names of seasonal festivals as appropriate. ◆W6◆

Read the poem 'Weather' on page 79.

Watchpoints

◆W1◆ *At set times on one day, observe the sun's changing position in the sky. Note how shadows lengthen or shorten at particular times.*

◆W2◆ *Not everyone's lifestyle follows the same pattern (for example, some people work at night). You could review Unit 1, Lesson 9 here.*

◆W3◆ *Are there certain things which always tend to happen on particular days in the week, for example, Brownies on Tuesdays, swimming on Thursdays?*

◆W4◆ *Seasonal characteristics are listed on page 100.*

◆W5◆ *Divide the children into four groups. Each group is to go on the same walk, but concentrate on using a different sense: listening, looking, touching, smelling.*

◆W6◆ *Diwali, Hanukkah, Christmas are winter festivals. Holi and Easter are spring festivals. See page 102 for further ideas.*

Learning outcomes

- ◆ All should know that there are regular cycles in our lives; daily, weekly, monthly, seasonal. They will be able to name the four seasons in order.
- ◆ Some may be able to list a range of the different characteristics of each season.
- ◆ A few will know that some religious festivals are particularly linked to certain seasons and be able to name some.

Life Cycles

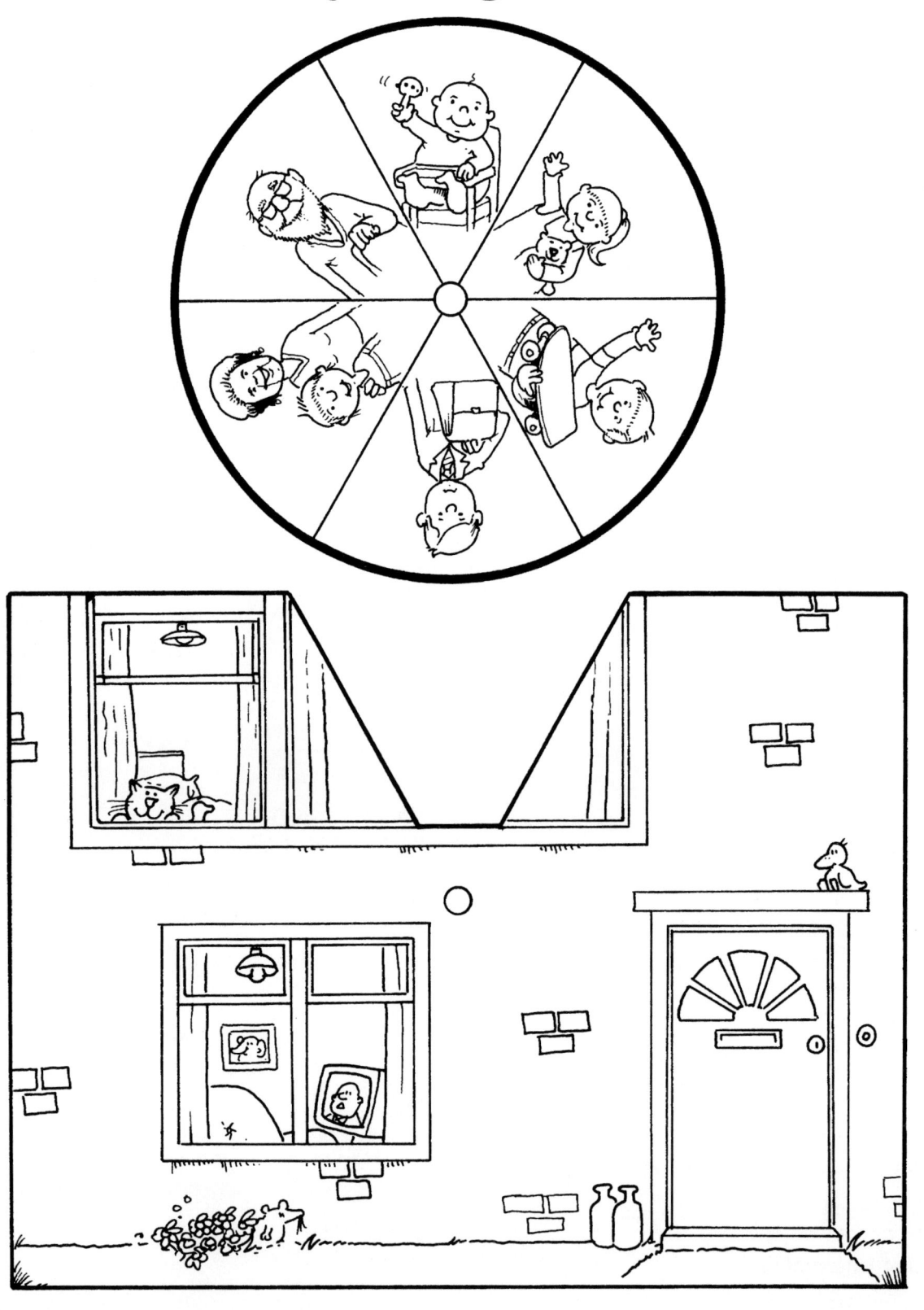

- Stick this sheet on to thin card.
- Cut out the two pieces.
- Fix the circle behind the house scene with a paper fastener
- Turn the circle to see the stages in the life cycle.
- What changes do you notice at each stage?

Key concept Beliefs, values, ultimate questions

Key words Birth, change, death, develop, heaven, life cycles, reincarnation, stages

Resources ◆ PS15 Life Cycles ◆ Card, glue, paper fasteners, scissors ◆ Story 'Ben and his Dog' (page 81) ◆ Videos, stories or pictures of examples of growth and change from the animal world.

UNIT 2

New Life

LESSON 5

Life Cycles

Background

In nature there are clearly discernible life cycles. What happens when we die is one of life's big questions. Buddhists believe that they will have to pass through many other lives before they can reach 'enlightenment', just as they believe the Buddha did. He taught that there was an 'Eightfold Path' for all to follow that will help people eventually to reach enlightenment.

Focus Buddhism/Christianity

Starting points

Discuss the changes that a caterpillar goes through before becoming a butterfly. Paint pictures of each of the stages and sequence them. Use videos, stories or pictures to reinforce this with examples of growth and change from the animal world, for example, the 'Ugly Duckling', birds and eggs, tadpoles to frogs.

Activities

Ask children to consider the ways in which they have grown and changed since they were born. How are they different now? Ask the children to suggest some of the stages we go through in our lives (for example, baby, toddler, schoolchild, teenager, adult, middle-aged person, old person). **W1**

Ask each child to use PS15 'Life Cycles' and make the pin wheel. Ask how people change as they grow up. What 'special' things happen at each stage? What would they like to do when they are grown up? Ask children what they think the good things and bad things about being grown up are. How is the human life cycle similar to other animals' life cycles? Explain simply what Buddhists believe about life and death. If the children could choose, what would they wish to be born as? **W2**

Development

Read the short story of 'Ben and his Dog' (page 81). Ask children what 'heaven' means to them. Explain briefly what Christians believe about death. **W3**

Watchpoints

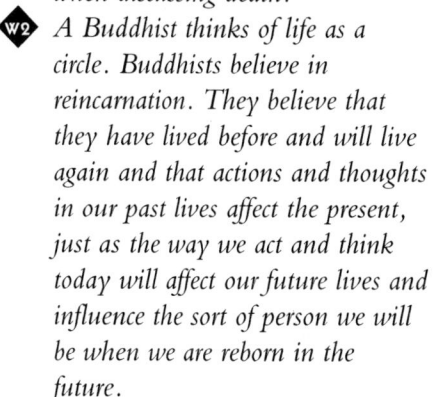

W1 *Consideration needs to be given to the personal experiences of children when discussing death.*

W2 *A Buddhist thinks of life as a circle. Buddhists believe in reincarnation. They believe that they have lived before and will live again and that actions and thoughts in our past lives affect the present, just as the way we act and think today will affect our future lives and influence the sort of person we will be when we are reborn in the future.*

W3 *Christians believe that death is not the end of existence. They believe that after death the souls of believers go to be with Jesus in heaven. The words of Jesus (John 11.25–26 from the Good News Bible) say, 'Those who believe in me will live, even though they die; and all those who live and believe in me will never die.'*

Learning outcomes

◆ All should know that all animals have life cycles, and describe one of them in reasonable detail.
◆ Some may be able to name some of the human developmental stages. They should also know that Buddhists believe in reincarnation.
◆ A few may be able to explain what Christians believe about life after death.

41

Flower Power

☆ Colour in the flower.
☆ Write your name in the middle.
☆ Cut out the flower.
☆ Fold the petals into the middle of the flower along the dotted lines.
☆ Put some water in a washing up bowl or sink.
☆ Float your flower on top of the water, with its petals facing upwards.
☆ Watch it open!

Key concept Symbolism, ultimate questions

Key words Bean, bulb, flower, growth, plant, potential, seed, tree

Resources
- PS16 Flower Power
- Story 'Johnny Appleseed' (page 88)
- Variety of things for growing (see Activities below)

UNIT 2

New Life

LESSON 6

Growing Things

Background

Over the years humans have marvelled at the potential of tiny seeds to grow into large plants and trees. Some faiths explain this by reference to a 'Creator God' who created the Earth and all that is in it. The suggestions below should be carried out over a period of time.

Focus General/Christianity

Starting points

Read and discuss the story of Johnny Appleseed (page 88). **W1**

Use PS16 'Flower Power' to encourage a sense of excitement and wonder about the potential of growing things

Activities

Growing things in class. Select one of the suggestions below. **W2** Think about the signs of new life as the plants begin to sprout, grow and develop. Parallels could be drawn to us as humans, the potential that is within each of us, and how we grow physically (and in other ways) given the right environment, care and nurture.

Mustard and cress seeds. Sprinkle some seeds on to cotton wool or tissues. Keep these moist (but not over watered).

Beans. Place some blotting paper, or paper tissues, in a glass jar and place a few beans between the paper and the inside of the jar so they can be seen. Keep the paper moist. **W3**

Bulbs and flowers. Plant bulbs or flower seeds at an appropriate time. This could be done in a flower tub or window box.

Development

Ask children what the purpose of trees is. List their ideas. Observe a tree that is near your school over a period of time. Record changes in writing and drawings. Study the tree for all its dependants – all life in, under and around it. Leaves could be collected and studied using magnifying lenses. Leaf rubbings and prints could be made. Different leaf shapes could be compared. Make a simple family tree. **W4**, **W5**

Watchpoints

- **W1** *Johnny Appleseed lived in America around the turn of the century.*
- **W2** *Use the suggestions to encourage a sense of wonder at the potential for growth within small seeds, beans or bulbs. Can this be explained? Who put this potential there? This presents many opportunities to record observations through discussion, writing, drawing or artwork.*
- **W3** *Do not use kidney beans as they can be toxic.*
- **W4** *Be sensitive to children's family backgrounds.*
- **W5** *In the Bible considerable store is set on the ancestry of great people. The family tree of Jesus is often shown as a tree springing from Jesse, the father of David.*

Learning outcomes

- All should be able to describe their experiences of growing some form of plant.
- Some may know that some religions believe in a 'creator God' and be able to explain what conditions are necessary to enable plants to grow.
- A few may be able to draw parallels between the growing potential of humans and plants and the sort of environmental conditions which enable this to be realised.

Sam's Baptism

People give Sam gifts and have a special party.

Sam's Mum and Dad take Sam to the church.

Sam's parents promise to help Sam learn to be a Christian.

The minister makes a sign of a cross on Sam's head with water.

Key concept Belonging, commitment, symbolism

Key words Baby, baptism, birth, ceremony, christening, church, font

Resources ◆ PS17 Sam's Baptism ◆ Poem 'My Baby Brother' (page 78) ◆ Notes on Hindu birth ceremonies (page 99)

UNIT 2

New Life

LESSON 7

Babies

Background

Infant baptism (or christening) is a way of welcoming babies into some denominations of the Christian church. Some denominations simply dedicate babies with a service of thanksgiving. Baptism may then be performed when the person is an adult. At the service the parents and godparents promise to help the child grow up as a Christian. The minister says prayers for the child and family, and names the child with the name the parents have chosen.

Focus Christianity/Hinduism

Starting points

If possible, ask a mother to bring in a new-born baby and talk about him or her to the class. Ask children to bring in photographs of themselves as babies. ◆W1 Arrange a display of them and have a 'Guess Who?' competition. Read the poem 'My Baby Brother' (page 78). In what way are all babies 'special'? Talk about the wonder and beauty of new babies.

Consider the custom of giving gifts to babies. Recall the story of Sleeping Beauty and the gifts the Good Fairies gave her such as beauty and happiness. Ask the children what special gifts they would like to give a baby.

Activities

Describe what happens when a baby is baptised. ◆W2
Ask children to cut out the pictures on 'Sam's Baptism' sheet and put them in the correct order. Ask them to draw a present they would give Sam and to make one wish for her. Encourage children to share their experiences and knowledge of such ceremonies and occasions. ◆W3

Development

Discuss the gestation period and how babies grow and develop inside their mothers. ◆W4 What happens to a woman during pregnancy? ◆W5

Watchpoints

◆W1 *Make sure the photographs are named on the back.*

◆W2 *The minister sprinkles water from a stone basin, called a font, over the infant's forehead, and makes the sign of the cross, to remind people of Jesus. The water symbolises being washed clean of sin. Sometimes a special candle is given to the parents of the child representing Jesus as the Light of the World.*

◆W3 *Details of Hindu birth ceremonies and customs are on page 99.*

◆W4 *See if any of the children's parents have a scan of their baby before it was born.*

◆W5 *The baby grows, the woman gets bigger, there are visits to the doctor and hospital for check-ups, etc.*

Learning outcomes

◆ All should be able to say why a new-born baby is special and know that some Christian families have their babies baptised (or christened).
◆ Some may be able to describe a Christian infant baptism in detail, and know that other faiths have similar birth and naming ceremonies.
◆ A few may be able to explain some of the symbolism involved in a Christian baby's baptism.

Holi Stick Puppets

Hiranyakasipu	Prahlad	Holika
The fire	An elephant	The snakes
Vishnu, as a lion	A soldier	A servant

- Enlarge on the photocopier
- Stick the sheet on to card.
- Colour the puppets
- Cut round the puppets.
- Stick them on to lollipop sticks
- Use them to tell the story of Holi.

Key concept Symbolism, belonging

Key words Celebrate, festival, fire, Hindu, Holi, Holika, Lord Krishna, Prahlad

Resources
- Poster 7
- PS18 Holi Stick Puppets
- Lord Krishna (page 89)
- Prahlad and Holika (page 94)

UNIT 2

New Life

LESSON 8

Holi

Focus Hinduism

Background

Holi is a Hindu Spring festival. It usually lasts around three days. The celebrations may consist of processions and floats. Significant characters such as Lord Krishna are portrayed in different ways. Stories and traditional songs are sung around fires. Holi is a time for making peace after quarrels and offering friendship. There is much feasting and eating of special sweets and foods. Special Holi bonfires are sometimes lit.

Starting points

Ask children about their experiences of fire.

What lively festivals or celebrations have they been to? Ask the children to talk about things they think are fun to do.

Activities

Look at the poster together. **W1** Ask children to describe what is happening. Tell them about the Hindu festival of Holi. Read the stories about Prahlad and Holika, and Lord Krishna (pp 89 and 94). Use PS18 'Holi Stick Puppets' as a way of helping children to re-tell and act out the story of Prahlad and Holika. **W2**

Development

Make a big picture of a bonfire. Encourage the children to mix and use fire colours of red, yellow and orange. Use crepe and cellophane paper. Have showers of sparks going up into the sky. Dab the paper with glue and sprinkle silver glitter over the glue spots to represent the sparks. The children could paint or draw themselves dressed up in party clothes and stick themselves around the 'Holi' fire. Any other written work or drawings about the topic could be pinned around the fire too.

Invite the children to wave coloured crepe paper streamers to represent a fire. Have your own 'Holi' celebration. Teach children the traditional greeting of 'Namaste'. **W3**

Watchpoints

W1 *On the second day, the Festival of Colours, people throw coloured paints over each other and young people play tricks on their elders. This reminds them of stories of Prince Krishna. Children could make a drop and splash painting by soaking white paper, and carefully sprinkling powder paint on to it. As it lands, the colours run into each other.*

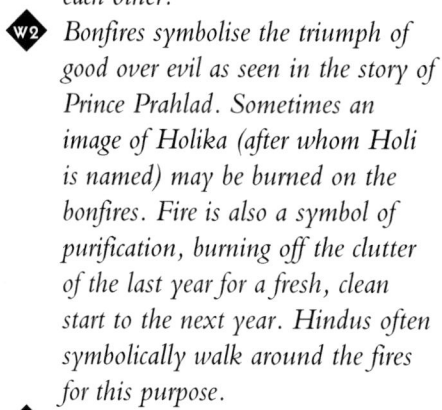

W2 *Bonfires symbolise the triumph of good over evil as seen in the story of Prince Prahlad. Sometimes an image of Holika (after whom Holi is named) may be burned on the bonfires. Fire is also a symbol of purification, burning off the clutter of the last year for a fresh, clean start to the next year. Hindus often symbolically walk around the fires for this purpose.*

W3 *Hindus greet each other by placing palms together and bowing – greeting the god in each other.*

Learning outcomes

- All should know Holi is a Hindu festival and describe some of the things people do to celebrate it. They will be able to retell something of the story of Prahlad and Holika.
- Some may be able to relate some of the celebrations to the stories of Prahlad and Holika and Lord Krishna and explain their origins.
- A few may be able to explain the meaning and symbolism of fire in the Holi festival.

The Easter Story

Key concept Authority, inspiration, commitment, beliefs, values

Key words Buried, cross, crucified, Easter, Good Friday, Jerusalem, Jesus, Last Supper, Palm Sunday, Pharisees, Romans, rose again, tomb

Resources
- Poster 8 ◆ PS19 The Easter Story
- Story 'The Mother Hen and her Chicks' (page 90) ◆ 'The Easter Story' (page 84)

UNIT 2

New Life

LESSON 9

The Story of Easter

Background

Easter is seen by Christians as one of the most important Christian festivals. It is a time when Christians remember the death of Jesus and rejoice that he rose again. Many Christians prepare for Easter during the forty day period of Lent which precedes it, starting on Ash Wednesday. Some Christians give up something they particularly like or enjoy during Lent as a reminder of the sacrifice Jesus made for them. On Palm Sunday, the beginning of Holy Week, Christians remember when Jesus entered Jerusalem. Maundy Thursday is the day on which Jesus shared the Last Supper with his disciples. Good Friday is the day when Jesus was crucified. Easter Sunday is a day of great joy and celebration. Christians believe Jesus rose from the dead on this day.

Focus Christianity

Starting points

Ask children to think of things that make them sad. Then ask them for things that make them happy. **W1**

Read and discuss the story of 'The Mother Hen and her Chicks' (page 90). **W2**

Activities

Read the story of Easter to the class in two parts (page 84). After Part 1 the Palm Sunday episode could be acted out in class. **W3** After Part 2 show children the poster and ask them to describe what they see and what they understand of it. **W4**

Use PS19 'The Easter Story'. Ask the children to sequence the pictures correctly and write a simple caption for each picture. Use the pictures to help them re-tell the story in their own words.

Development

Make a display of work on the Easter story. At the centre could be a large plain cross, symbolising the risen Christ. **W5** Children's work could be displayed around the outside of the cross. The pictures from the photocopiable sheet could be enlarged and used.

Watchpoints

- **W1** *Easter is a time of both sadness and happiness for Christians.*
- **W2** *This story may help children understand better that Christians believe Jesus was prepared to give his life for them.*
- **W3** *Paper palm leaves could be made by folding and cutting for waving.*
- **W4** *The cross is a potent symbol to all Christians reminding them of the sacrifice Jesus made for them. The empty tomb is a sign of hope and joy because Jesus promised to be with them always. '... and I [Jesus] will be with you always, to the end of the age.' (Matthew 28.20)*
- **W5** *Many Christians think of Jesus as an invisible friend. The empty cross reminds them of this.*

Learning outcomes

- ◆ All should know that Easter is a Christian festival and be able to retell some of the Easter story.
- ◆ Some may be able to retell the Easter story in detail and in the correct sequence.
- ◆ A few may be able to explain some of the deeper meaning and significance of Easter to Christians.

Easter Cards

Key concept Symbols, belonging

Key words Candle, cross, customs, eggs, Holy Week, new life, symbol

Resources ◆ PS20 Easter Cards ◆ Notes on pre-Easter period (page 99) ◆ Materials for activities (see below) ◆ Hot cross bun recipe (page 99) ◆ White candle

UNIT 2

New Life

LESSON 10

Easter Customs and Symbols

Background

The beginning of 'Holy Week', Palm Sunday, is a day of processions, when people wave palm leave to remind them of Jesus' entry to Jerusalem. On Good Friday people eat hot cross buns which carry the symbol of the cross. Easter Sunday is full of joy and happiness. Christians greet each other saying 'Christ is risen'. Churches are bedecked with flowers which symbolise new life and hope. Easter cards are exchanged and Easter eggs are given.

Focus Christianity

Starting points

Ask children to suggest things they associate with Easter. Discuss how different people celebrate Easter. ◆W1

Go through the significance of the sequence of days in Holy Week (above) and the period leading up to it (pp 99–100).

Activities

Eggs. Decorate the shells of hard-boiled eggs with felt tips, or by sticking on sequins and glitter. The eggs may be made into different faces. ◆W2

Crosses. Ask children where crosses may be seen. Make crosses out of strips of paper or make potato prints using cross patterns. Make and eat some hot-cross buns (see page 99 for recipe). ◆W3

Candles. Use white wax candles for drawing cross patterns on plain paper. Wash over the paper with a light paint wash and watch the crosses magically appear! ◆W4

Easter cards. Make Easter cards. Include symbols of new life on them such as those on PS20 'Easter Cards'. Encourage the children to compose a suitable Easter message inside, perhaps using the words 'Christ is risen'.

Development

Have a quiet time of reflection. Use a candle to light the room. ◆W5 Talk quietly to the children about of the Easter story. Allow a time for quietness and silence.

Watchpoints

◆W1 *Some people: go to church; give eggs, cards or flowers; have a holiday; visit friends; dress up in best clothes, etc.*

◆W2 *The egg, as well as being a symbol of new life is also a reminder of the shape of the stone that was rolled away from the mouth of the tomb, allowing life to break free from its darkness.*

◆W3 *The cross reminds Christians of Jesus' sacrifice.*

◆W4 *Huge 'Paschal' candles are lit in churches on Easter Sunday as a symbol of light and life beating back the powers of darkness and death.*

◆W5 *The candle reminds Christians of Jesus whom they call the Light of the World, and how he defeated the darkness of death and rose again.*

Learning outcomes

◆ All should know that Easter is a Christian festival. They will be able to name at least one of the symbols associated with Easter.

◆ Some may be able to name three symbols related to Easter and be able to explain something of their meaning. They will have some idea of the chronology of the events of Holy Week.

◆ A few may have a clear idea of the meaning behind most of the symbols used at Easter and be able to recount some details about the forty day period preceding Easter.

STANLEY THORNES
infant RE

UNIT 3

SPECIAL BOOKS

INTRODUCTION

All faith communities have sacred writings and holy books. This unit is designed to help children appreciate that religious books and writings communicate experiences, ideas and information and offer followers of that faith a code to live by.

During the course of this unit, children will learn about the Bible, Qur'an and Torah and something of their importance to religious individuals and faith communities. Children will learn something of the origins and characteristics of these writings, and how they are used and treated. Children will also learn through stories, about some key figures associated with each book.

Unit 3 – Overview

Lesson	Contents	Key Concepts	Religious Focus
1	**I Like Books** Books are generally perceived by our society as having an important role in the life and education of children. ◆ What sort of books do children like? ◆ What sort of books are there? ◆ What purpose do they serve?	Authority, inspiration	General
2	**Telling Stories** Many pre-literate societies placed great emphasis on transmitting information, beliefs and traditions by word of mouth (and still do). Many sacred writings were originally passed on orally before being written down. ◆ Which stories do we remember? ◆ Do we learn anything from stories? ◆ What are the difficulties of passing things on orally?	Authority, inspiration, belonging	General
3	**Religious Books** All the world's major faiths have some form of sacred writings. By producing their own class book, children can gain insights into religious books in general. ◆ What characteristics do religious books have? ◆ What sort of things do they contain? ◆ What sort of rituals are associated with them?	Authority, inspiration, belonging, symbolism	General

Lesson	Contents	Key Concepts	Religious Focus
4	**The Bible** The Bible is the Christian religious book. Part of it, the Old Testament, consists of the same collection of books from which Jewish holy writings are derived. ◆ What does the Bible represent to Christians? ◆ What does it contain? ◆ How has it been passed on over the years?	Authority, inspiration, belonging, symbolism	Christianity
5	**Jesus Calms the Storm** To Christians the life, death and teachings of Jesus are of pivotal importance. Jesus is at the very heart of the New Testament. This story, and the next, are based on events recorded in the Bible. ◆ What is this story all about? ◆ What does this story tell Christians about Jesus? ◆ How can a story like this help Christians today?	Authority, inspiration, symbolism	Christianity
6	**Jesus Heals a Blind Man** What sort of person was Jesus? ◆ What sort of things did he do? ◆ What message is there in the story for Christians?	Authority, inspiration, symbolism	Christianity
7	**The Torah** The Torah is the religious book of the Jewish faith. ◆ What do Jews believe the Torah to represent? ◆ What does it contain? ◆ How is it used?	Authority, inspiration, belonging, symbolism	Judaism
8	**Moses and the Ten Commandments** Moses is a key figure in Jewish history. He was a leader, a prophet and a lawgiver. This story tells how God imparted the Ten Commandments to him. ◆ What sort of person was Moses? ◆ What is the purpose of the Commandments? ◆ Why are they important to the Jewish people?	Authority, inspiration, lifestyle	Judaism
9	**Muhammad, God's Messenger** To Muslims, Muhammad is the last and most important prophet. This story tells how Allah (God) revealed His word through Muhammad (as codified in the Qur'an). ◆ Who was Muhammad? ◆ How did Allah reveal His word to him? ◆ What happened afterwards?	Authority, inspiration	Islam
10	**The Qur'an** The Qur'an is the religious book of the Islamic faith. ◆ What does it contain? ◆ How is it written? ◆ How is it used?	Authority, inspiration, belonging, symbolism	Islam

What's in it?

Which book has maps in it? ——————————

Which book tells you how
    to cook things? ——————————

Which book has information
    on dogs in it? ——————————

Which is a holy book? ——————————

Which is a story book? ——————————

Key concept Authority, inspiration

Key words Fiction, holy books, information, library, non-fiction, story, words relating to books

Resources
- PS21 What's in it?
- Variety of different types of books (see under Activities)

UNIT 3

Special Books

LESSON 1

I Like Books

Focus General

Background

Books may serve different functions and purposes, such as to entertain, to inform, to explain. Most sacred books contain a variety of types of writing encapsulating beliefs and values. Many books, especially sacred books, are seen as having some sort of authority vested in them.

Starting points

Ask the children what books they like. Why do they like them? Why do people read books? Look at a couple of different books. What can be learned from the covers, date of publication, contents and index pages? Ask children to suggest ways we should care for books and look after them; handling them properly, not leaving books on the floor, not tearing them or writing in them, not folding pages, storing them properly in the correct place. **W1**

Activities

Hold up a story book and an information book. What is the same about each? (Both have covers, text and pictures, etc.) What is different? (The purpose – to entertain or to inform.) Introduce the terms 'fiction' and 'non-fiction'. **W2**

Collect together a range of different sorts of books. **W3** Hold each one up. Ask children what sort of a book it is and what its purpose is (for example, to explain things). Play the 'What Book?' game. For example, 'If I wanted to find someone's telephone number which sort of book would I look in?' Use PS21 'What's in it?' Ask which of these sorts of books they have got at home. Ask if they know the names of any holy books.

Development

Make a display of children's 'special' or 'favourite' books. Have a 'Book of the Week' or 'Favourite Author' table. Have a 'Design a Cover' competition. Get each child to make a simple book of their own. **W4** Visit the school or local library to consider how it is organised. Draw attention to the way books are grouped into fiction and non-fiction and discuss other age-appropriate library skills like alphabetical order, etc. Ask children to try and find particular types of books, for example, religious books and stories. **W5**

Watchpoints

W1 *In most faiths holy books are treated with great reverence and respect.*

W2 *All major faiths have some form of sacred scriptures. Holy books tend to be written with adult, rather than child, readers in mind. Most faiths have one or more holy books which contain a variety of different types of writing including stories, history, information and explanation.*

W3 *For example, story book, poetry book, diary, cookery book, dictionary, telephone directory, a comic, a holy book (the Bible).*

W4 *Book-making provides many opportunities for talking about different aspects of books. Choose from the ideas on page 100.*

W5 *The Dewey classification for religious books is 200-299.*

Learning outcomes

- All should be able to name their favourite book and know that there are many different types of books, including holy books.
- Some may be able to explain the differences between books according to their purpose and function.
- A few may be able to name some holy books and where to find them in the library.

How Will it End?

What happens next?

Key concept Authority, inspiration, belonging

Key words Change, memory, word of mouth, written,

Resources ◆ PS22 How Will it End? ◆ Sequences of pictures telling a story

UNIT 3

Special Books

LESSON 2

Telling Stories

Background

Many pre-literate cultures relied on oral story-telling for passing on information, beliefs and traditions (and some still do). This places great reliance on the accuracy of re-telling and memory. Some disadvantages are that the original may be subtly altered or interpreted in different ways in the re-telling.

Focus General

Starting points

Ask the children who tells them stories. Ask what stories they remember best. Why? What kind of things do people tell stories about? Do stories have to be true? Why do people tell stories? Can we learn anything from stories? **W1** Ask children to think of all the different types of stories they can. Choose one category, say fairy stories. Ask what sort of things you find in a fairy story. **W2** Ask what sort of things they would expect to find in holy books.

Activities

Ask the children if a story is only a proper story if it is written down. Discuss the fact that many stories are told and passed on by word of mouth and not written down. Does this matter? **W3**

Ask the children to tell the story of what they did last weekend. Do we tell everything that happened? Which bits do we leave out? Why? Do we always tell it exactly as it happened? **W4**

Play Chinese whispers to demonstrate how we rely on memory and interpret things differently. Try PS22 'How will it end?'. Ask children to work in groups of three. Get each child to make up a different ending. Child A then tells their ending to Child B, who then repeats Child A's ending to Child C. Child A listens to see how accurate it is.

Development

Chain stories: provide the opening few sentences. The children take it in turns to add to and finish the story.

Picture sequences: provide groups of children with a set of four to six pictures, which, when sequenced, tell a story. Each group has to decide which order they go in and make up a story. Compare stories and see how different the stories can be using the same basic ingredients.

Watchpoints

◆ **W1** *Many stories in holy books have a message or are trying to teach us something.*

◆ **W2** *Settings: castle, palace, woods, mountains, caves. Characters: King, Queen, Prince, Princess, dragon, frog, unicorn, witch, giant. Events: Magic spells, getting lost, being captured and rescued, happy endings.*

◆ **W3** *In some cultures the tradition of oral story-telling is still very strong. The holy scriptures of many faiths were initially transmitted orally prior to being written down.*

◆ **W4** *In story-telling there is a tendency to be selective, and to rely on our memory to a great extent. Also in telling and listening we tend to filter things through our own experiences. They may then become subject to our personal interpretation.*

Learning outcomes

◆ All should know that stories may be told or written down and may or may not be true.
◆ Some may know that some stories have been passed on by word of mouth for many years.
◆ A few may be able to explain some of the problems involved in passing on information orally and know that some holy books were originally passed on by word of mouth before being written down.

About Me

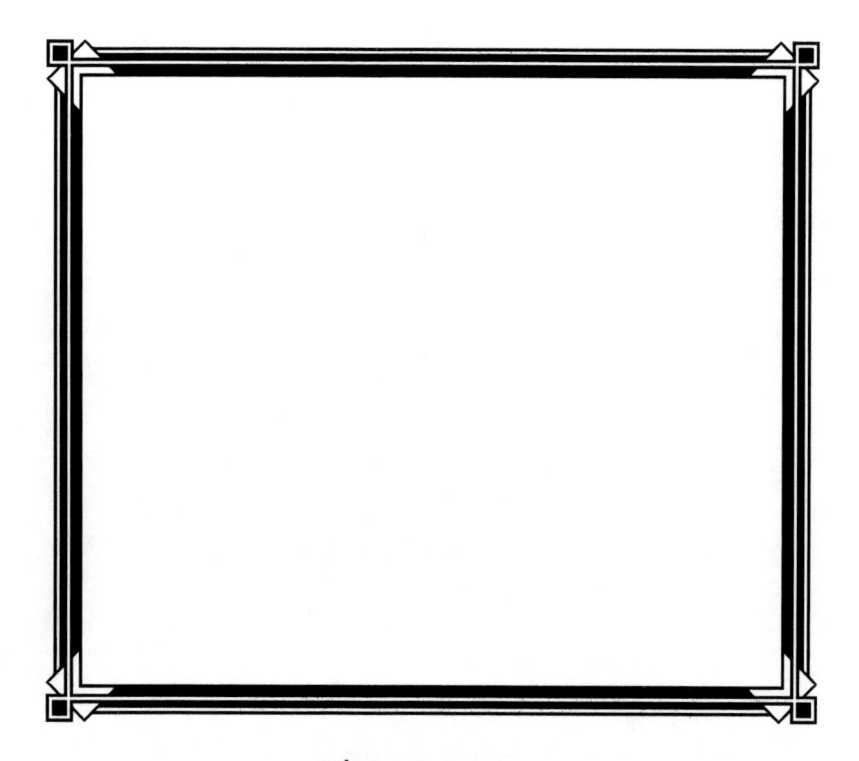

My name is ―――――――――――――――

This is me

Here are five interesting things about me.

1 ―――――――――――――――――――
2 ―――――――――――――――――――
3 ―――――――――――――――――――
4 ―――――――――――――――――――
5 ―――――――――――――――――――

Draw or glue on a photograph of yourself.

Write five things about yourself.

Key concept	Authority, inspiration, belonging, symbolism
Key words	Faith, history, holy, religion, respect, special, value
Resources	◆ PS23 About Me and PS1 I am Special

UNIT 3

Special Books

LESSON 3

Religious Books

Background

All the world's major faiths have some form of sacred writings. They may contain beliefs, a code for living and explanations to life's big questions. They may be in the form of stories, teachings, letters, wise sayings, rules, history, songs, poems and prayers. Whatever form sacred books take they are very important to the followers of that faith.

Focus General

Starting points

Ask children what things they have at home that are very old, special or precious. Discuss the concept of 'value'. Do they have any really expensive or valuable books at home? How are these treated? Where are they kept? Are they allowed to look at them? Ask children how the family recalls family memories. Do they talk about them? Do they have a family photograph album? Videos? Are these valuable?

Activities

Explain that the class is going to produce a special class book which will tell others what the class is like. Include in the book details of a communal class experience (for example, a trip, a party, something special the class is all involved in); a piece of personal writing from each child (you could use PS23 'About Me' or PS1 'I am Special' for this); some classroom rules. Once these have been produced, discuss: how will it be decorated and bound? How will it be kept safe, clean and available? Where will it be kept? How often will it be read? Who will be able to read it? Who else will be told about it? Whose responsibility will it be to look after it? Have a special day to celebrate its completion. **W1**

Development

Look for books with a 'history' in school, for example, the School Log Book. Find out what they contain. Explain that most faith communities (religions) have special holy books. Draw parallels between the class book and sacred (holy) books. **W2**

Watchpoints

W1 *This activity is intended to help children gain some insight into the characteristics of sacred books. Pupils will gain some idea of the sort of writings sacred books may contain, the fact that there are often rituals associated with them, and that they may be treated with respect.*

W2 *The scriptures of many religions are the words of wise or holy people about God. They may be used by people worshipping alone or in groups. They may be beautifully decorated or plain. Holy Books may contain information about individuals and what they think, history of important events, guidance and rules on how to live. They are often beautifully presented and treated with respect.*

Learning outcomes

- ◆ All should know that many people treat holy books with care and respect.
- ◆ Some may be able to state the contents of their class book and explain why it is special.
- ◆ A few may be able to name some holy books and draw some parallels between the class book and the holy books.

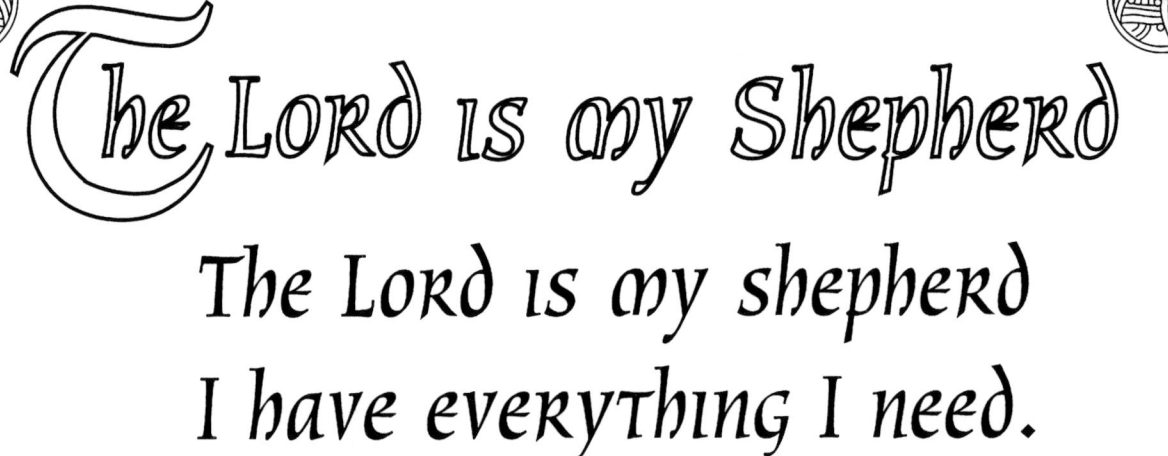

The Lord is my Shepherd

The Lord is my shepherd
I have everything I need.

Key concept Authority, inspiration, belonging, symbolism

Key words Bible, Christian, God, Jesus, library, Testament

Resources
- ◆ PS24 The Lord is my Shepherd ◆ Poster 9
- ◆ Copy of Bible (if possible two different versions) ◆ Letter in envelope ◆ Torch
- ◆ PS33

UNIT 3

Special Books

LESSON 4

The Bible

Focus Christianity

Background

To Christians the Bible provides a guide for their faith, belief and way of living. It is divided into two sections. The *Old Testament* is the same collection of books which form the Jewish holy books. Christians believe that the Old Testament shows how God revealed himself, guided the Jewish people, and gave them laws and leaders. The *New Testament* tells the story of Jesus and the beginnings of the worldwide early Church. Christians see it as the beginning of a new relationship between God and humanity.

Starting points

Show children a Bible (or preferably have a display of several different versions of the Bible). Find out the extent of the children's current knowledge about the Bible. Show the children a letter in an envelope. Ask children to guess who it is from. Ask why people send letters (to say something important, to send a message, etc.). Take out a torch and ask what it is for (to guide us, to help us see, to show us the way, etc.). Ask how many children have Bibles at home. Explain that many Christians use Bibles to help them learn more about God in their daily lives. **W1**

Activities

Ask children what a library is. Discuss how it works, how the books are classified and organised. **W2**

Ask children if they can name any stories or books from the Bible. Discuss any stories they suggest.

Look at and discuss the poster. Ask children to colour and decorate the verse from the Bible on PS24 'The Lord is my Shepherd' and add their own picture. **W3**

Christians treat the Bible with respect and love. Explain that many churches keep a special Bible to be read from which is often kept on a special stand (lectern) (see PS33, page 76). **W4**

Development

Ask children how people in other countries, who speak different languages, are able to read the Bible. **W5**

Read and compare a passage from the King James Version with a passage from the Good News Bible. **W6**

Watchpoints

W1 *Christians think of the Bible as a letter from God, containing his message to them, and as a light sent by God.*

W2 *The Bible has 66 books written by different people at different times. It contains laws, history, songs, letters, stories, prophecies and poetry.*

W3 *Before printing was invented copies of the Bible were lovingly, carefully and beautifully hand-written by monks.*

W4 *The Bible is used extensively in church services for reading, reflection, prayer and teaching.*

W5 *The Bible has been translated into over 2,000 languages. The eagle on the lectern in many churches symbolises the word being carried to every part of the world.*

W6 *There are many different versions of the Bible in English.*

Learning outcomes

- ◆ All should be able to say that the holy book of Christians is the Bible.
- ◆ Some may be able explain why the Bible is like a library and name the two major parts of the Bible.
- ◆ A few may be able to explain why Christians treat the Bible with love and respect.

Jesus Calms the Storm

☆ Colour and cut out the boat and the two pictures of Jesus.

☆ Stick them on to lollipop sticks.

☆ Use them to help you re-tell the story.

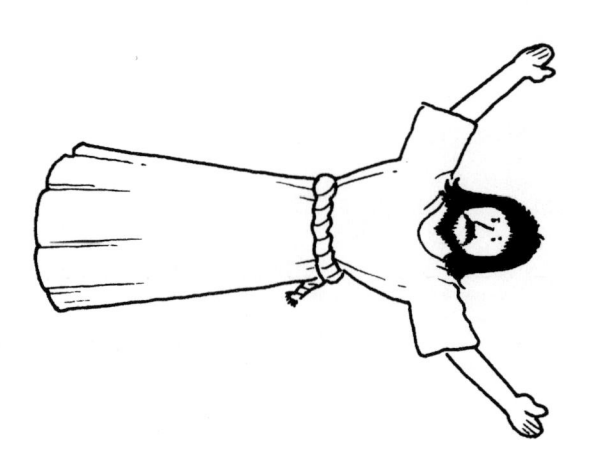

Key concept Authority, inspiration, symbolism

Key words Calms, depend on, faith, Jesus, storm, trust

Resources
- Poster 10 ◆ PS25 Jesus Calms the Storm
- Story 'Jesus Calms the Storm' (page 86)
- Lollipop sticks, glue, a long strip of paper, paints

UNIT 3

Special Books

LESSON 5

Jesus Calms the Storm

Background

To Christians the life, death and teachings of Jesus are of pivotal importance in the Bible. Their belief that God came to the world in the human form of Jesus, is at the heart of the New Testament. Christian beliefs are founded on Jesus' example, events in his life and his teachings both directly and through stories he told.

Focus Christianity

Starting points

Ask the children to talk about times when they have been frightened, such as at night, starting a new school, being lost, during a storm, etc. What was it that frightened them? What did they do? Who did they turn to for help and reassurance or comfort? Ask children to list people they trust such as parents, friends, teachers, doctors. What makes these people trustworthy? What sort of people don't they trust? Why not?

Activities

Look at the poster. Ask children to say what they think is happening. Can they guess what happened before or what will happen after? Read and discuss the story 'Jesus Calms the Storm' (on page 86). **W1**

Have children complete PS25 'Jesus Calms the Storm' and use the stick puppets and boat to re-tell the story. Have Jesus asleep on the boat at the beginning then change to the figure of Jesus rebuking the storm at an appropriate point in the story. **W2**

Development

We all need to place trust in others at times. Play the 'Blindfold Game'. Blindfold a child and help him or her move around the room, avoiding all the obstacles, with verbal instructions only. Discuss how a baby completely depends on an adult for everything and how blind people build up a great trust and dependence on their guide dogs. **W3**

Watchpoints

W1 *Weather conditions can change very rapidly on the Sea of Galilee. The storm in this story, however, must have been particularly fierce because many of Jesus' disciples were fishermen and would have been used to facing all sorts of weather conditions.*

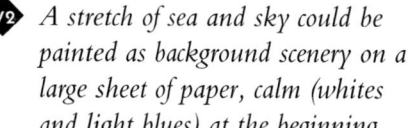

W2 *A stretch of sea and sky could be painted as background scenery on a large sheet of paper, calm (whites and light blues) at the beginning, stormy (dark blue, grey, black and whites) in the middle and calm at the end.*

W3 *Christians believe Jesus is interested in their everyday lives and situations. This Bible story shows Christians the supernatural power of Jesus and that he is someone they can have faith, trust and confidence in.*

Learning outcomes

- ◆ All should be able to re-tell the story in reasonable detail.
- ◆ Some may be able to relate the story to a time in their own lives when they were frightened and name some people they trust.
- ◆ A few may be able to explain what the story shows about Jesus and how Christians believe this can help them today.

63

I Am Glad I Can See

Key concept	Authority, inspiration, symbolism
Key words	Blind, care, concern, cured, disabled, faith, healing, power
Resources	◆ PS26 I Am Glad I Can See ◆ Story 'Jesus Heals a Blind Man' (page 86) ◆ White wax candle

UNIT 3

Special Books

LESSON 6

Jesus Heals a Blind Man

Background

Christians learn about Jesus through the Bible. The Bible talks about Jesus' teachings and lifestyle, as well as his actions and miracles performed by him. Christians believe that the story of Jesus healing the blind man underlines both his human concern and his supernatural miraculous powers.

Focus Christianity

Starting points

Find out what common illnesses the children have had. Perhaps some have had a more serious illness. How did they feel? Were they frightened? Who looked after them? Who helped them? Did they ever feel they weren't going to get better? Ask the children what they think it would be like to be permanently disabled in some way – for example, if they were in a wheelchair, or blind. **W1**

Activities

Read the story 'Jesus Heals a Blind Man' (page 86). Ask children what sort of a life they think Bartimaeus led most of the time. **W2** Act out the story.

Development

Ask children to write thank-you prayers for something they are grateful for. Ask each child to draw one beautiful thing they are glad they can see on PS26. Compile a 'Book of Beautiful Things' from their drawings. Take a sheet of white paper and write the name of Bartimaeus on it with a white wax candle. Wash over it with a colour wash. Explain this is what it might have been like for Bartimaeus suddenly to see things. **W3**

Find and read other stories about Jesus healing. What help is available for blind people in our society?

Watchpoints

W1 *Be sensitive to any children in the class who suffer from permanent disabilities.*

W2 *In Bible times people thought that serious illness was a punishment for something the person, or one of their predecessors, had done. There was no medical help or social security and so the disabled were obliged to beg. Generally they were despised and avoided by the majority.*

W3 *Jesus is often called 'The Light of the World'. Becoming a Christian is often spoken of as 'seeing the light'. Christians may see this story as symbolic in this respect.*

Learning outcomes

◆ All should be able to re-tell the story in reasonable detail.
◆ Some may be able to explain something of the life Bartimaeus may have led and what this story tells us about his faith.
◆ A few may be able to explain what the story shows about Jesus and the sort of person he was.

The Torah

- Kippah
- Ark
- Yad
- Prayer shawl
- Torah scroll

Key concept Authority, inspiration, belonging, symbolism

Key words Ark, breastplate, crown, Jewish, parchment, pointer, rabbi, scroll, synagogue, Torah

Resources ◆ PS27 The Torah ◆ Ready prepared 'Torah' (see Activities below) ◆ Lollipop sticks, paper

UNIT 3

Special Books

LESSON 7

The Torah

Focus Judaism

Background

The Torah is considered the most important of the Jewish scriptures and consists of the five books of Moses. It is seen as the authority for all Jewish teaching. The Jews believe the Torah embodies God's laws, is a guide to living and tells the history of God's special relationship (covenant) with them. The Torah is treated with great reverence and respect.

Starting points

Ask the children to look at PS27 and describe what they see. Through discussion explain why the Torah is special to the Jewish people. What are the physical characteristics of the Torah? W1 How is it written? W2 Where is it kept? W3 What it is used for and who uses it? W4

Activities

Make a simple scroll. Have the words of the Shema written on it (these can be found on PS28). W5 Cover the scroll you have made with a decorative cloth and silver foil 'breastplate'. Have a foil 'crown' attached to the top of each handle of the scroll. Re-enact a reading from the Torah. Have the children stand silently and the 'rabbi' (Jewish priest) carry the scroll around the 'congregation'. At the front of the class the 'rabbi' should ceremoniously lay the scroll on a 'special' table, and 'undress' the scroll. A selected member of the class should come to the front and, using a special 'pointer' read from the scroll. Follow the reading by a discussion of what this reading might mean. Allow the children to make their own small 'Torah' scrolls (use lollipop sticks as the handles), covers, breastplates and pointers. Use PS27 'The Torah' to consolidate some important points about the Torah.

Development

Celebrate the festival of Simhat Torah (the birthday of the Torah). Make flags and sing and dance in a procession as the 'Torah' scroll is carried around the room seven times. Ask a different child to carry the 'Torah' on each circuit of the room. Follow this by a special party. W6

Watchpoints

W1 The Torah is in the form of a scroll, and is written on parchment. It is is covered with a decorative cloth (a 'mantle'). A silver breastplate hangs in front of it (like that originally worn by the High Priest). At the top of each wooden pole of the scroll is a silver crown.

W2 Copies of the Torah are hand-written in Hebrew.

W3 The Torah is kept in a special cupboard (the Holy Ark) as a reminder of the Ark of the Covenant in which the Ten Commandments were originally kept.

W4 The Torah is used for worship and study. When it is being read a special pointer (a 'yad', often made of silver) is used to avoid actual contact with the Torah.

W5 The Shema is a Jewish prayer affirming belief in one God and comes from the book of Deuteronomy 6.4–5.

W6 The festival of Simhat Torah celebrates the end of one year and the beginning of the next in the reading of the Torah.

Learning outcomes

◆ All should know that the Torah is the holy book of the Jews.
◆ Some may be able to detail some of the physical characteristics of the Torah.
◆ A few may be able to explain why the Torah is important to the Jewish people and how it is used.

A Mezuzah

☆ Stick this template onto thin card. Cut it out. Make a mezuzah.

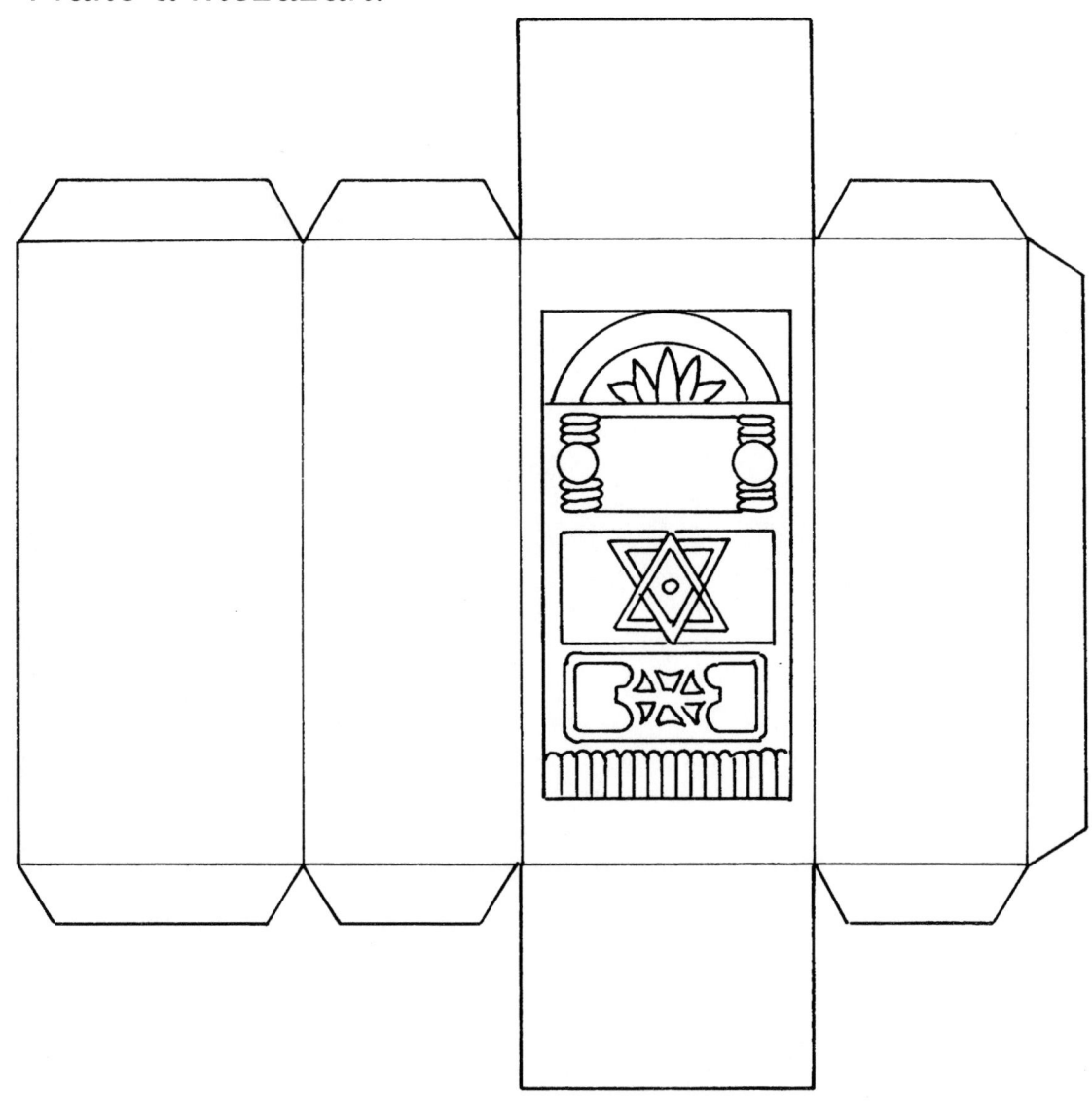

☆ Cut out the Shema. Roll it up like a scroll. Put it inside the mezuzah.

Hear O Israel, the Lord our God is one God. You shall love the Lord our God with all your heart, soul and strength.

Key concept Authority, inspiration, lifestyle

Key words Commandments, God, Israelites, mezuzah, Moses, obey, rules, Shema

Resources ◆ Story 'Moses and the Ten Commandments' (page 89) ◆ PS28 A Mezuzah ◆ PS34 Moses and the Ten Commandments

UNIT 3

Special Books

LESSON 8

The Ten Commandments

Background

Moses was responsible for shaping the character of the nation of Israel. He led the Israelites out of Egypt and God chose to impart the Ten Commandments to him. These form the basis of God's Law on right living. The Torah consists of the five books of Moses W1

Focus Judaism

Starting points

List some of the games children play. Choose one of them, like snakes and ladders. Ask them to explain the rules of the game. Do all games have rules? Why? How do some people break the rules? What happens when the rules get broken? Name some of the rules for traffic on the road, for example, keep left, speed limits, wearing seat belts, traffic lights. Do we need these rules? Why? What happens if they are broken? Who makes the rules at home or when playing games in the playground? Ask the children who they obey (for example, parents, teachers, referees). Why?

Activities

Ask if anyone knows anything about Moses. Tell them a little about him and why he is very special. W2 Explain that the story about Moses is from the Torah (and also the Bible) and is about God's Rules. Read and discuss the story of Moses and the Ten Commandments (page 89), using PS34, page 77. Get each child to make a mezuzah using PS28 'A Mezuzah'. W3

Development

Ask the children to discover more about Moses' birth and life before this story. Does the class have any rules? What rules would make it a better place? Ask the children to contribute one rule each they think is important. Make a class list of ten different rules. Do the children have any rules at home? Who makes them? What rules do they have?

Watchpoints

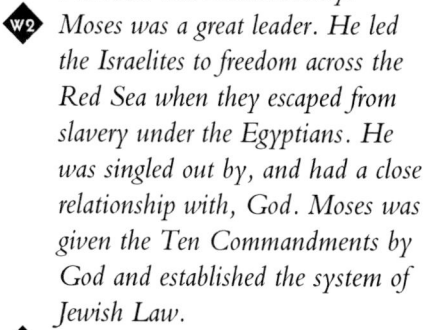

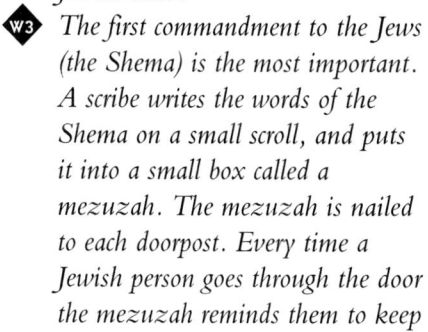

W1 *Genesis, Exodus, Leviticus, Numbers and Deuteronomy.*

W2 *Moses was a great leader. He led the Israelites to freedom across the Red Sea when they escaped from slavery under the Egyptians. He was singled out by, and had a close relationship with, God. Moses was given the Ten Commandments by God and established the system of Jewish Law.*

W3 *The first commandment to the Jews (the Shema) is the most important. A scribe writes the words of the Shema on a small scroll, and puts it into a small box called a mezuzah. The mezuzah is nailed to each doorpost. Every time a Jewish person goes through the door the mezuzah reminds them to keep God's laws.*

Learning outcomes

◆ All should be able to re-tell the story in reasonable detail.
◆ Some may be able to explain what a mezuzah is and what it contains.
◆ A few may be able to list some of the Ten Commandments.

Notice

☆ Draw a sign and write a notice.

Key concept Authority, inspiration

Key words Allah, Angel Gabriel, Arabic, Makkah, memorise, message, messenger, Muhammad (pbuh), prophet, Qur'an

Resources ◆ Poster 11 ◆ Muhammad (pbuh), God's Messenger (page 91) ◆ PS29 Notice

UNIT 3

Special Books

LESSON 9

Muhammad (pbuh) – God's Messenger

Background

Muslims believe Muhammad was the last and most important prophet. Whenever Muslims mention the name of the Prophet Muhammad, they always also say 'Peace be upon him' as a mark of respect (see page 5). In written English this is abbreviated to the initials 'pbuh'. They believe it was through him that God revealed his word as encapsulated in the Qur'an. **W1** It was through Muhammad that Islam became an established world faith and the Qur'an was written.

Focus Islam

Starting points

Look at the poster. Use this as a stimulus for discussing how messages are sent and received. **W2** Ask children for their ideas on how we might get messages from God (prayers, dreams, holy books, holy people, etc). Many people believe that there have been some very special messengers from God, called prophets. Can the children name any? For example, Jesus or Moses.

Activities

Read and discuss the story 'Muhammad (pbuh), God's Messenger' (page 91). Explain that Muslims consider him to be a most special messenger from Allah. **W3**

Explain that Muslims do not make pictures of Muhammad or the angel because Muslims believe that all living things are made by Allah and it is wrong to try to imitate his work.

Development

How do we remember things? (Writing a note, asking someone to remind us, putting it on the calendar. Is it hard to remember things? Try playing the memory game 'I went to market and bought ...'. Each child in turn says the phrase and suggests an item to be bought. The next child has to repeat this and add another item, etc. How far does it get before it breaks down? Why? What special ability did God give to Muhammad? Ask children what other things they can discover about Muhammad. **W4**

Watchpoints

W1 *The first revelation of the Qur'an to Muhammad is known as the Night of Power (Laylat-ul-Qadr). The Night of Power is celebrated on one of the last ten nights of Ramadan.*

W2 *For example, messages from nature (black clouds, leaves falling from trees); written messages (letters, lists, signs, adverts, newspapers, books); spoken messages (talking, TV, radio, telephone); non-verbal messages (road signs, hand signal). Children could design and display their own signs and notices on PS29 'Notice'.*

W3 *The Muslim name for God is Allah. The first pillar (fundamental belief) of Islam, states 'I bear witness that there is no god but Allah and I bear witness that Muhammad is His servant and His messenger.'*

W4 *Muhammad is believed to have memorised the whole of the Qur'an which consists of 114 chapters or suras.*

Learning outcomes

◆ All should be able to re-tell the story of Muhammad in reasonable detail.
◆ Some may be able to explain why Muhammad is so important to Muslims.
◆ A few may be able to explain what a prophet is.

The Qur'an

☆ These words are in Arabic which is written from right to left.

☆ They say 'Allahu Akbar' which means 'Allah is most great'.

☆ Colour round them carefully and then colour in the patterns around them.

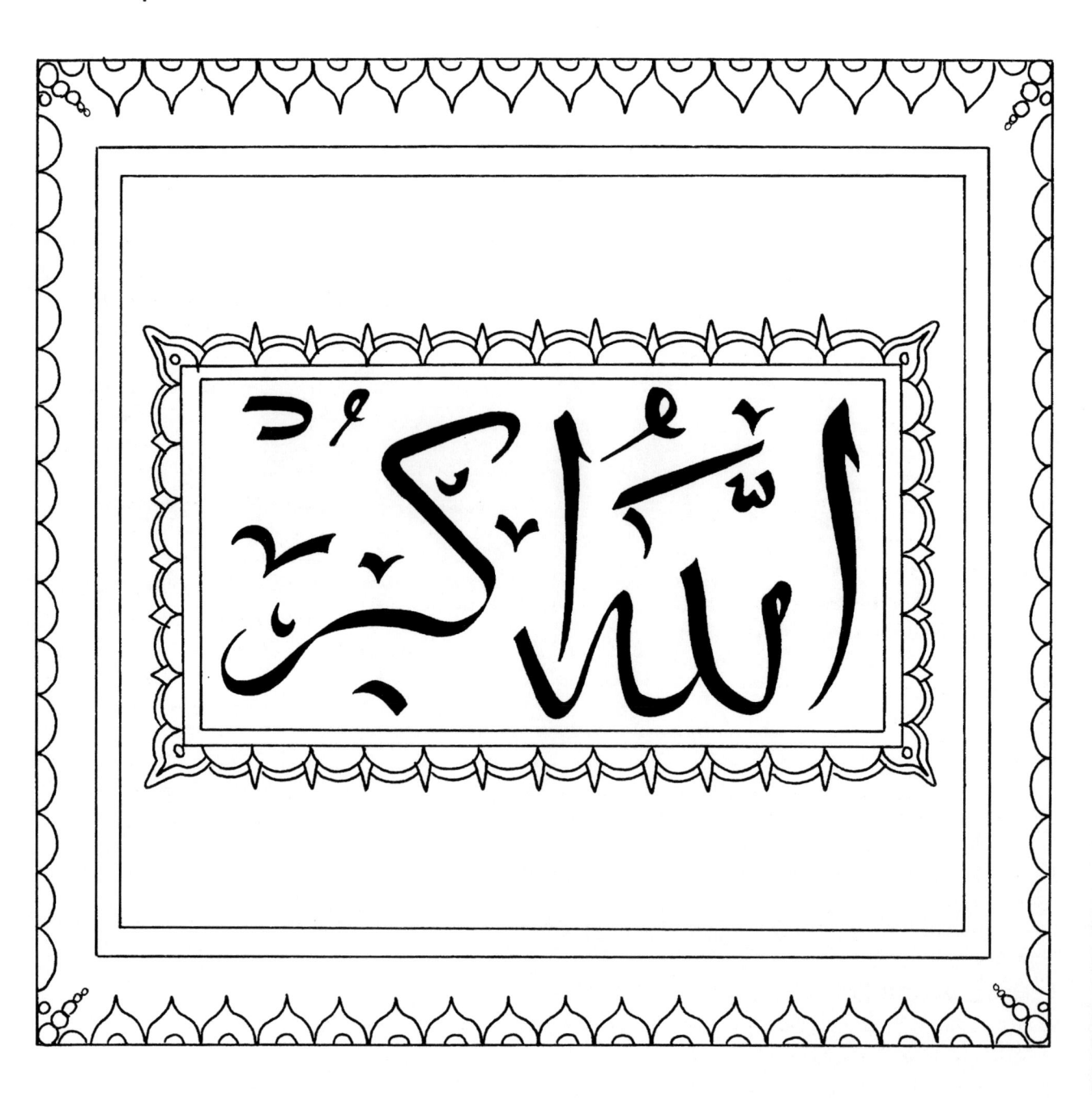

Key concept Authority, inspiration, belonging, symbolism

Key words Allah, Arabic, Muhammad (pbuh), Muslim, Qur'an, respect

Resources ◆ Poster 12 ◆ PS30 The Qur'an

UNIT 3

Special Books

LESSON 10

The Qur'an

Background

The Qur'an, a sacred Islamic writing, is believed by Muslims to be the word of God (Allah) revealed to the prophet Muhammad (pbuh). It forms the basis of the laws of many Islamic countries. The Qur'an forms a very important part of daily worship, praise and prayer. According to Islam the Angel Jibril (Gabriel) revealed the words of God to Muhammad. He memorised the words and recited them to his friends and followers. After his death they wrote them down, producing the first Qur'an in approximately 650 CE.

Focus Islam

Starting points

Ask the children to choose a favourite book which is special to them. For example, their 'baby' book containing records of their first few months, the first book they had, a nursery rhyme book, etc. Ask why the book has special meaning to them.

Activities

Show the poster. Ask children to talk about what they can see. Through discussion explain why the Qur'an is special to Muslims, what is in it, how it came to be written, what it is used for and who uses it. Show a copy of the Qur'an. Ask children how they handle very special, precious things. Put the book on a stand or special table. Ask the children to wash their hands before coming to look at the book. **W1** Explain why the Qur'an is written in Arabic. **W2** Explain that Arabic is written from right to left. If possible, have someone talk or write in Arabic. **W3** Explain why such care is often taken with the decoration and writing in the Qur'an. Ask children to colour the Arabic writing and patterns on PS30 'The Qur'an'. Explain that the words say Allahu Akbar which means 'Allah is most great'. **W4**

Development

Provide a short, beautiful poem for the children to recite and try to learn by heart. **W5** Think of ways of making a bookstand for a special book. Ask children to find out more about the Prophet Muhammad.

Watchpoints

W1 *The Qur'an is treated with enormous respect and reverence. A person must wash thoroughly before handling it. It is placed on a stand when being read to keep it off the floor and prevent it from being handled too much.*

W2 *Arabic the language in which the Qur'an was revealed. Many believe that translating the words would affect their meaning.*

W3 *Muslims whose first language is not Arabic, study Arabic at a mosque, school or home.*

W4 *Since Muslims believe the words to be those spoken by Allah, the Qur'an is often written in beautiful calligraphy. It may be decorated with Islamic patterns but no pictures.*

W5 *Muslims today place a lot of emphasis on memorising whole sections of the Qur'an. The word Qur'an actually means 'the recitation'.*

Learning outcomes

- ◆ All should know that the Qur'an is an Islamic holy book.
- ◆ Some may be able to explain that Muslims believe the Qur'an to be the actual words of Allah (God) as revealed to the Prophet Muhammad.
- ◆ A few may be able to list some ways which demonstrate how the Qur'an is treated with respect.

How do they feel?

What made them feel like this?

What might their feelings make them do?

Muslim Prayer Timetable

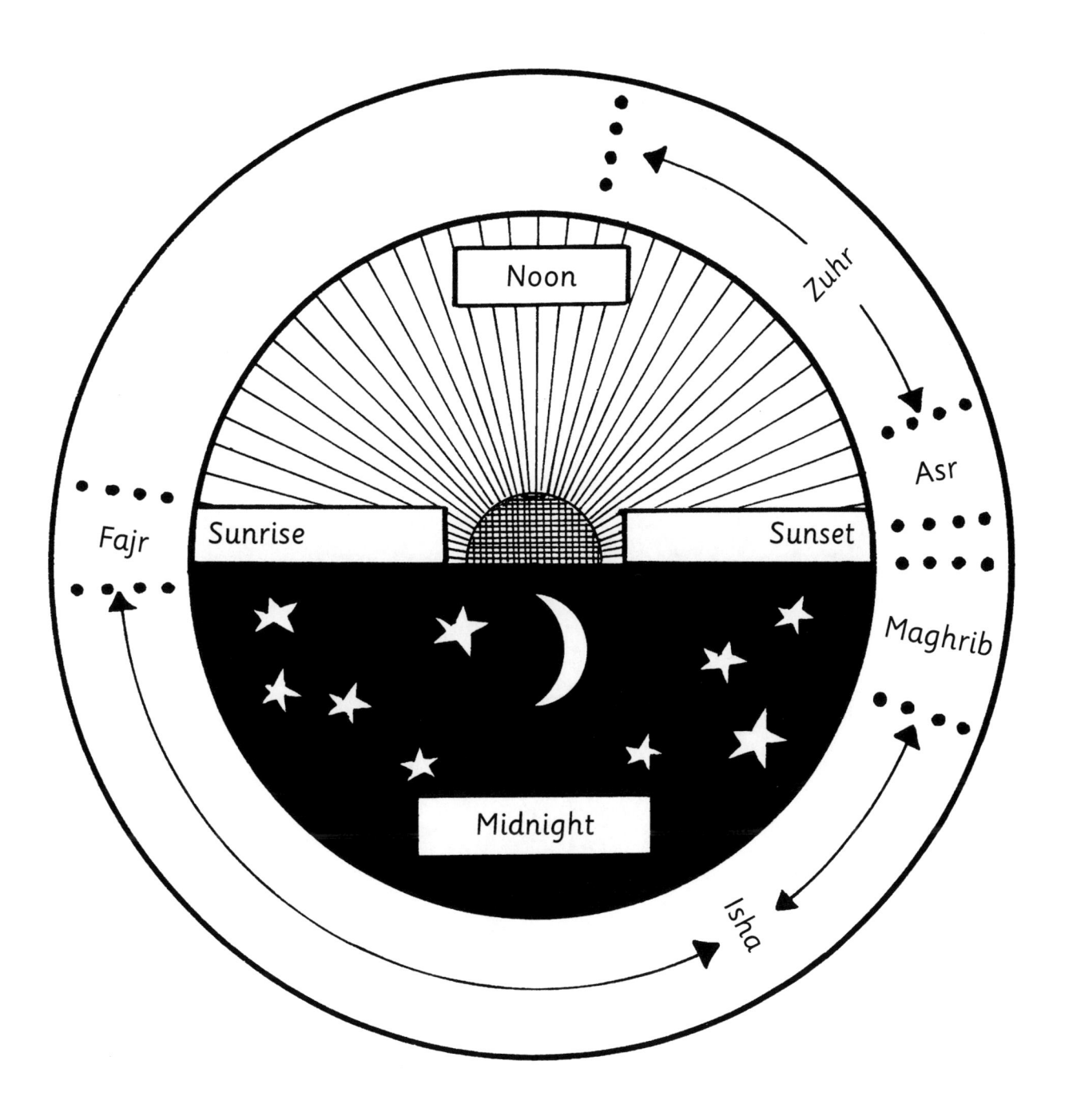

- Noon
- Sunrise
- Sunset
- Midnight
- Fajr
- Zuhr
- Asr
- Maghrib
- Isha

The Bible

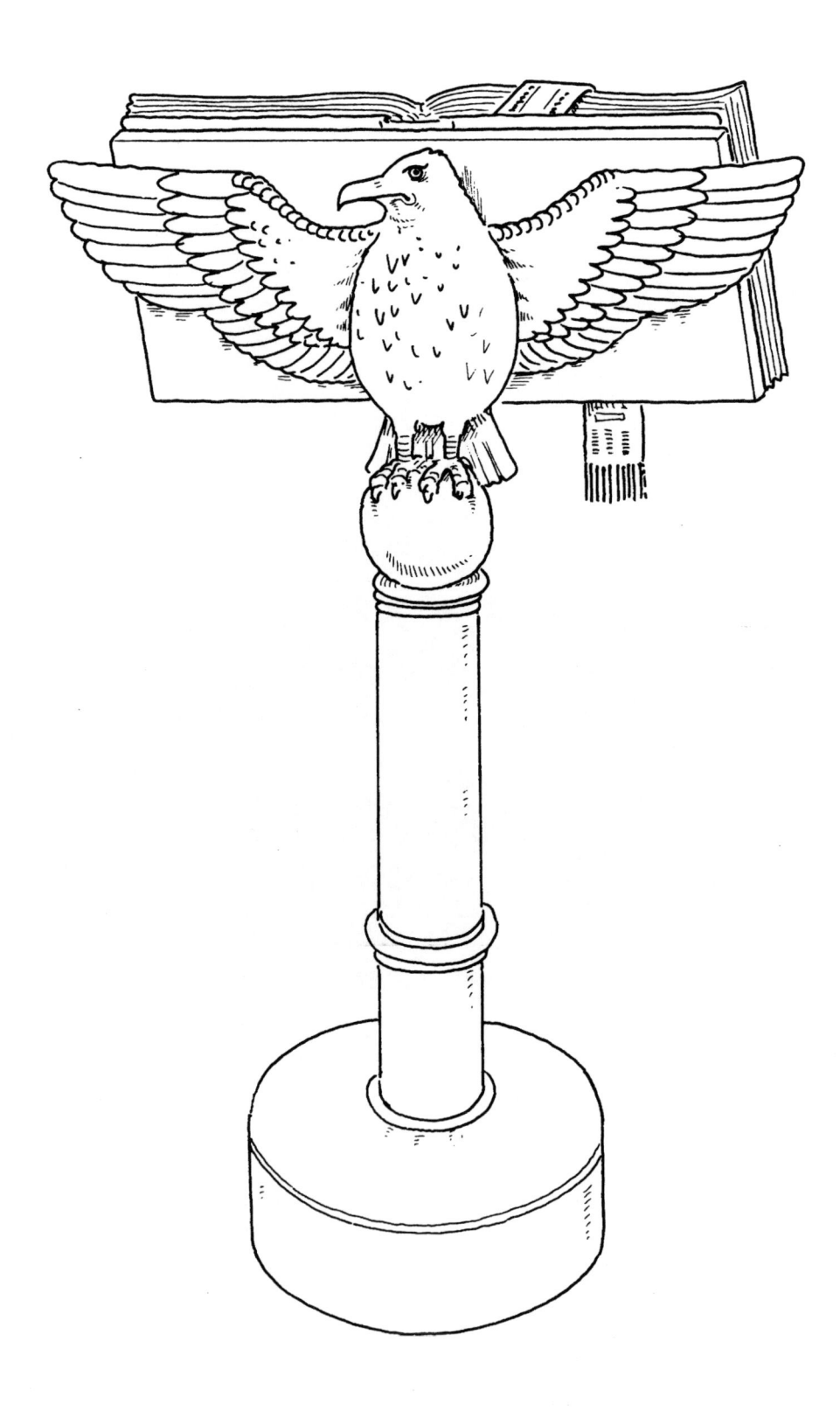

Moses and the Ten Commandments

Poems, Songs and Prayers

A Buddhist Prayer

I will do all the good I can,
In all the ways I can,
In all the places I can,
At all the times I can,
As long as ever I can,
Thank you, Lord Buddha.

Lord Buddha is with me.

My Baby Brother

My baby brother's beautiful,
So perfect and so tiny.
His skin is soft and velvet brown;
His eyes are dark and shiny.

His hair is black and curled up tight;
His two new teeth are sharp and white.
I like it when he chews his toes;
And when he laughs his dimple shows.

Mary Ann Hoberman

Our Family Comes From Around The World

Our family comes
From around the world:
Our hair is straight,
Our hair is curled,
Our eyes are brown,
Our eyes are blue,
Our skins are different
Colours, too.

>   Tra la tra la
>   Tra la tra lee
>   We're one big happy family!

We're girls and boys,
We're big and small,
We're young and old,
We're short and tall.
We're everything
That we can be
And still we are
A family.

>   O la dee da
>   O la dee dee
>   We're one big happy family!

We laugh and cry,
We work and play,
We help each other
Every day.
The world's a lovely
Place to be
Because we are
A family.

>   Hurray hurrah
>   Hurrah hurree
>   We're one big happy family!

By Mary Ann Hoberman

Think of a World Without any Flowers

Think of a world without any flowers,
Think of a world without any trees,
Think of a sky without any sunshine,
Think of the air without any breeze.
We thank you, Lord,
    for flowers and trees and sunshine,
We thank you, Lord,
    and praise your holy name.

Think of a world without any animals,
Think of a field without any herd,
Think of a stream without any fishes,
Think of a dawn without any bird.
We thank you, Lord,
    for flowers and trees and sunshine,
We thank you, Lord,
    and praise your holy name.

Think of a world without any people,
Think of a street with no one living there,
Think of a town without any houses,
No one to love and nobody to care.
We thank you, Lord,
    for flowers and trees and sunshine,
We thank you, Lord,
    and praise your holy name.

          Words by DOREEN NEWPORT

The Sun Wakes Up

The sun wakes up
Yes, the sun wakes up.

The sun it smiles
Yes, the sun it smiles.

The wind it blows
Yes, the wind it blows.

The clouds come over
Yes, the clouds come over.

The rain falls down
Yes, the rain falls down.

The earth dries up
Yes, the earth dries up.

The sun lies down
Yes, the sun lies down.

The dark moves in
Yes, the dark moves in.

The moon looks up
Yes, the moon looks up.

The night lies still
Yes, the night lies still.

The sun wakes up
Yes, the sun wakes up.

          JOHN RICE

Weather

January, new beginning, resolutions, snowflakes spinning.
February, frosty fogs, winter shivers, fire-warm logs.
March blows windy, smells of spring, leaves peek out, brave blackbirds sing.
April showers fall soft and slow, earth wakes up and green things grow.
May Day ribbons round a pole, May-time babies, lamb and foal.
June brings summer blazing in, scent of roses, sun on skin.
July joy means school is out, time for picnics, heat and drought.
August goes on holiday, sandy castles, friends to stay.
September sees the autumn come, plough the fields one by one.
October gales lash the trees, leaves a-swirling, crashing seas.
November nights all crisp and cold, winter coats for young and old.
December dark, yet full of light, Christmas carols, star so bright.

          By LUCY COATS

What Can I Give Him?

What can I give him,
As poor as I am?
If I were a shepherd,
I would bring him a lamb.
If I were a wise man,
I would do my part;
Yet what I can give him –
Give my heart.

CHRISTINA ROSSETTI (1830-94)
This is part of the Christmas carol, 'In the Bleak Midwinter'.

Who Put the Colours in the Rainbow?

Who put the colours in the rainbow?
Who put the salt into the sea?
Who put the cold into the snowflake?
Who made you and me?
Who put the hump upon the camel?
Who put the neck on the giraffe?
Who put the tail upon the monkey?
Who made hyenas laugh?
Who made whales and snails and quails?
Who made hogs and dogs and frogs?
Who made bats and rats and cats?
Who made everything?

Who put the gold into the sunshine?
Who put the sparkle in the stars?
Who put the silver in the moonlight?
Who made Earth and Mars?
Who put the scent into the roses?
Who taught the honey bee to dance?
Who put the tree inside the acorn?
It surely can't be chance?
Who made seas and leaves and trees?
Who made snow and winds that blow?
Who made streams and rivers flow?
God made all of these.

Words and music by PAUL BOOTH

Stories

BEN AND HIS DOG

Ben loved Kim, his pet dog. Kim was a small West Highland Terrier and was full of life. She would run down the path to meet Ben when he came home at lunchtimes to feed her. Ben and Kim loved nothing better than to roll around the floor playing. Ben took Kim for long walks. Kim loved chasing other dogs and was always getting up to mischief.

One day, when Ben came home, he was surprised because Kim did not run up the path to meet him. When he went indoors, Kim was lying in her basket, and barely lifted her head. Ben knew something was wrong. 'Mum! Mum!' he called. 'Come quick!'

Ben's Mum came downstairs and took Ben in her arms. 'Kim's not well,' she said. 'She hasn't been right all morning. It must be her age. She's not getting any younger, you know. When Dad comes home tonight we'll take her to the vet.'

The vet looked at Kim and said sadly, 'I'm sorry. There's nothing I can do. Kim's had a good life, but she's old now and her body doesn't work as well as it used to. She's very lucky to have such a loving family as you to look after her.' Ben bit back the tears. He knew what the vet said was right. He knew in his heart that Kim was dying. No one spoke in the car on the way home. Everyone was too sad.

Kim died peacefully in her sleep three days later. Ben was broken-hearted and cried for hours. The family decided to have a special ceremony for Kim. Ben wrote a short prayer and put it in a special box, along with some of Kim's hair and a photgraph of her as a puppy, to be a constant reminder of what a lovely dog she had been. 'Even though she's dead, she's still alive in my memory,' sobbed Ben. 'Nothing can change that.'

◆ *Ask the children what sort of feelings Ben would have had when his pet died.*

THE CHRISTMAS STORY

(as told in the *Good News Bible*)

Part 1 – The Birth of Jesus

Matthew 1.20–21
... An angel of the Lord appeared to him in a dream and said, 'Joseph, descendant of David, do not be afraid to take Mary to be your wife. For it is by the Holy Spirit she has conceived. She will have a son, and you will name him Jesus – because he will save his people from their sins.'

Luke 2.1–7

At that time the Emperor Augustus had ordered a census to be taken throughout the Roman Empire. When this first census took place, Quirinius was the governor of Syria. Everyone, then, went to register himself, each to his own town. Joseph went from the town of Nazareth in Galilee to the town of Bethlehem in Judea, the birthplace of King David. Joseph went there because he was a descendant of David. He went to register with Mary, who was promised in marriage to him. She was pregnant, and while they were in Bethlehem, the time came for her to have her baby. She gave birth to her first son, wrapped him in strips of cloth and laid him in a manger – there was no room for them to stay in the inn.

Points to discuss

◆ *God's promise that the baby was very special.*
◆ *The reasons for the journey to Bethlehem.*
◆ *The problems of finding accommodation.*
◆ *The humble surroundings in which Jesus was born.*

Part 2 – The Shepherds

Luke 2.8–20

There were some shepherds in that part of the country who were spending the night in the fields, taking care of their flocks. An angel of the Lord appeared to them, and the glory of the Lord shone over them. They were terribly afraid, but the angel said to them, 'Don't be afraid! I am here with good news for you, which will bring great joy to all the people. This very day in David's town your Saviour was born – Christ the Lord! And this is what will prove it to you: you will find a baby wrapped in strips of cloth and lying in a manger.'

Suddenly a great army of heaven's angels appeared with the angel, singing praises to God: 'Glory to God in the highest heaven, and peace on earth to those with whom he is pleased!'

When the angels went away from them back into heaven, the shepherds said to one another, 'Let's go to Bethlehem and see this thing that has happened, which the Lord has told us.'

So they hurried off and found Mary and Joseph and saw the baby lying in the manger. When the shepherds saw him, they told them what the angel had said about the child. All who heard it were amazed at what the shepherds said. Mary remembered all these things and thought deeply about them. The shepherds went back, singing praises to God for all they had heard and seen; it had been just as the angel had told them.

Points to discuss

◆ *The scene on the hillside, shepherds looking after their sheep at night.*
◆ *The bright light in the sky frightening the shepherds.*
◆ *The angel reassuring them, telling them the good news.*
◆ *The choir of angels singing praises to God.*
◆ *The shepherds, surprised at the news, go in search of the baby.*
◆ *The scene at the stable.*
◆ *Jesus – God's gift for everyone, young, old, rich or poor.*

Part 3 – The Wise Men

Matthew 2.1–11

Jesus was born in the town of Bethlehem in Judea, during the time when Herod was king. Soon afterwards, some men who studied the stars came from the east to Jerusalem and asked, 'Where is the baby born to be the king of the Jews? We saw his star when it came up in the east, and we have come to worship him.'

When King Herod heard about this, he was very upset, and so was everyone else in Jerusalem. He called together all the chief priests and teachers of the Law and asked them, 'Where will the messiah be born?'

'In the town of Bethlehem in Judea,' they answered. 'For this is what the prophet wrote: "Bethelehem in the land of Judah, you are by no means the least of the leading cities of Judah; for from you will come a leader who will guide my people Israel." '

So Herod called the visitors from the east to a secret meeting and found out from them the exact time the star had appeared. Then he sent them to Bethlehem with these instructions, 'Go and make a careful search for the child, and when you find him, let me know, so that I too may go and worship him.'

And so they left, and on their way they saw the same star they had seen in the east. When they saw it, how happy they were, what joy was theirs! It went ahead of them until it stopped over the place where the child was. They went into the house, and when they saw the child with his mother Mary, they knelt down and worshipped him. They brought out their gifts of gold, frankincense, and myrrh, and presented them to him. Then they returned to their country by another road, since God had warned them in a dream not to go back to Herod.

Points to discuss

- *The wise men studied the stars. They understood things from them.*
- *When they saw the new star and how it moved across the the sky they wondered what it meant.*
- *Their journey – the preparation, the choice of gifts, their expectations.*
- *The visit to King Herod. They expected the new king to be there.*
- *Their journey to Bethlehem.*
- *Arrival and presentation of gifts.*
- *How all these visitors and events must have confirmed to Mary and Joseph what a special baby Jesus was.*

THE CREATION

Based on the Bible story (Genesis, Chapters 1 and 2)

In the beginning everything was in darkness. There was no shape to the world – but God was there. There has never been a time when God did not exist. He existed even before the beginning of the world.

On the first day God said, 'Let there be light,' and there was light. God divided the light from the darkness and created night and day. God was pleased with his work.

On the second day, God made the sky. He made it like a huge dome over the Earth. God was pleased with his work.

On the third day God separated the waters from the land. God made dry land. He called this earth. On the earth he put grass, seeds and trees. He made the waters into seas and rivers. God was pleased with his work.

On the fourth day God made the sun to come out during the day and the moon at night. He also made all the stars for the sky. God was pleased with his work.

On the fifth day God made the fish and all other sea creatures for the deep blue sea. He filled the sky with birds. The sea and sky teemed with life. God was pleased with his work.

On the sixth day God made all the animals that live on the earth, from the smallest ant to the biggest elephant. Then God said, 'I will make human beings to take care of all the living things that I have made in the sky and sea and on land. I will make human beings in my likeness.' God made a man and called him Adam. Later on God made a woman called Eve as Adam's wife. He gave them a beautiful garden called Eden to live in. The garden had everything they needed. God was pleased with his work.

On the seventh day God rested. He blessed the seventh day and made it holy. Ever since then one in seven days has been a day when people can rest from their work.

THE EASTER STORY

Part 1 – Palm Sunday to the Last Supper

Based on the Bible story (Luke 19–22)

Jesus and his friends were on their way to Jerusalem. They were going to celebrate the festival of the Passover. Jerusalem was full of people at that time. Many had come from other places to visit their relatives. Many were hoping to see Jesus, for they had heard lots about the wonderful things he had said and done. They had heard that he was a great storyteller and teacher. There were even rumours that he had performed miracles – that he had made blind men see and cured people of all sorts of things. For years people had been waiting for a great leader to come and free them from the Romans who ruled them. Some thought Jesus could be this warrior king. Everyone was very excited. However, there were some people in Jerusalem who hated Jesus. The chief priests and Pharisees didn't like Jesus. Jesus often said outrageous things about God which they disagreed with. They planned to capture Jesus and take him prisoner.

It was a Sunday when Jesus and his followers reached Jerusalem. As Jesus entered the city the cheering crowds greeted him. They were just a little surprised that he was riding a donkey. Donkeys were thought of as peaceful animals. The crowds had expected Jesus to be riding a magnificent white horse, just like a warrior king. Still, they didn't let that spoil things. The crowds cheered and waved palm branches. Some people took off their cloaks and spread them on the road to walk over, just as they would have done for a king. 'Hosanna! Praise to God!' they shouted. Many were happy, but some in the crowd were not. Some of the city's religious leaders, the Pharisees, muttered amongst themselves. 'We must get rid of him,' they said. 'Who does he think he is, coming in and behaving in such a way?' They looked at Jesus with hatred in their eyes.

On the Thursday of that week, Jesus and his friends met together to celebrate the Passover and to have a special meal. Jesus really surprised them all when they came in. Their feet were all hot and dusty for they wore open sandals. Jesus sat them down and washed their feet with cool, refreshing water, just like a servant. Jesus said, 'You call me Lord, but I tell you that no one should be too important or proud to serve others. Follow my example when I'm gone. Do as I do. Love one another.'

During the meal there was a feeling of sadness amongst Jesus' friends because he told them that he would soon be leaving them. His friends did not understand it, but Jesus knew he was going to die. Jesus even told them that one of them would let them all down and give him away to their enemies. 'What do you mean?' they asked. 'We all love you.' But Judas said nothing. He knew Jesus was talking about him. He got up and walked out.

Some questions to discuss:

◆ *What can be learnt from Jesus when he washed his disciples' feet?*
◆ *How do you think Jesus knew he was going to die?*
◆ *How do you think the story will carry on?*

Part 2 Good Friday to Easter Sunday

Based on the Bible story (Matthew 26–28)

It was hot and stuffy in the room where they had eaten together, so later that evening they all went out into the cool air. They went to the Garden of Gethsemane, to pray. Whilst they were there, there was a sound of tramping feet. A group of Roman soldiers, carrying swords and clubs, marched up and grabbed Jesus. Judas had brought them, just as Jesus had said. Jesus' friends were so frightened that they ran off and left him on his own.

Jesus was taken to the house of Caiaphas, the high priest. Caiaphas and the other priests and teachers of the law tried hard to find fault with Jesus. They tried everything they knew to trick him. But Jesus just stood quietly and said nothing. The priests got angrier and angrier when they could find nothing to blame him for. At last they asked, 'Tell us – are you the Son of God?' Jesus said he was. 'How can you dare to say such a thing?' Caiaphas asked furiously. 'Put him to death!' the others shouted. But they did not have the power to do so. Only the Roman ruler could do this.

They dragged Jesus in front of the Roman Governor, a man named Pontius Pilate. He questioned Jesus but could find no reason to punish him. The priests and Pharisees were not satisfied. They wanted Jesus dead. In the end, just to satisfy them, the Governor agreed that Jesus should be killed. Jesus was taken away and cruelly beaten. Roman soldiers made fun of him. They even stuck a crown made of thorns on his head. They made him carry a huge, heavy, wooden cross to a hill outside the city. There they nailed him to the cross between two other crosses on which two thieves were also being crucified.

Crowds gathered and watched. Some of them were sad, but some of them mocked Jesus and made fun of him. 'You saved others,' they shouted. 'Why don't you save yourself?'

Jesus looked down on them with sadness and pity. 'Father, forgive them, for they don't know what they are doing,' he said. As Jesus was dying he gave a loud cry. Although it was the middle of the day the skies grew dark. The ground shook and the sky thundered. The Roman soldiers were frightened. One of them said, 'This man really was the Son of God.'

That evening, after he had died, Jesus was taken down from the cross by a man called Joseph of Arimathea. He wrapped Jesus' body in cloth and placed it in a cave-like tomb. A large heavy stone, too big for one man to move, was rolled across the entrance. Soldiers were sent to guard the tomb.

Early on Sunday morning Mary and some friends of Jesus came sadly to pray at the place where he had been buried. They saw that the stone had been rolled away and that the tomb was empty. They were very puzzled. What could have happened? Suddenly an angel appeared and said, 'Jesus is not here. He has risen from the dead!' The women were filled with happiness. They had thought that Jesus was dead – but now he was alive! They turned and raced to tell all their friends the good news. It was just as Jesus had said it would be.

Some questions to discuss:

◆ Why did Caiaphas and the priests want Jesus killed?
◆ What sort of man do you think Pontius Pilate was?
◆ Why do you think Jesus did not try to save himself?
◆ How do you think Mary and friends felt at the tomb?
◆ How could Jesus be alive?

JESUS CALMS THE STORM

Based on the Bible Story (Luke 8.22–25)

Jesus had been talking to the crowds all day. He was tired and needed a rest, so he got into the boat and asked his friends to sail across to the other side of the lake. By the time they were halfway across the gentle rocking of the boat had sent Jesus to sleep. Andrew looked down at him and smiled.

Just then a slight breeze tugged at Andrew's cloak. He shivered slightly and pulled his cloak around him to keep warm. As he looked up, Andrew saw dark clouds gathering in the sky. 'Looks like there's a storm on the way,' he said.
'I wouldn't be surprised at all,' Peter replied. 'You know how quickly the weather can change here.'

Just then spots of rain started to fall on the deck. Jesus still carried on sleeping, unaware of the rain. The wind picked up and the boat began to bob about more violently as the waves got bigger and rougher. John looked at Jesus anxiously. He was still sound asleep.

Soon the whole sky was black and the rain was coming down in sheets. Flashes of lightning streaked across the sky and peals of thunder boomed around the lake. The angry wind whipped up the water into huge waves. Jesus still did not wake up.

Jesus' friends were becoming more frightened. They were beginning to worry the boat would sink and that they would all be drowned. Peter could stand it no longer. He shook Jesus to wake him up. 'Save us! Save us!' he shouted.

Jesus rubbed his eyes and looked around. 'What's the matter?' he asked calmly. 'Why are you so frightened? Have you no faith?' He stood up, and lifted his hands into the air. The thunder seemed to roar and the wind howl louder. 'Be quiet!' he commanded the wind. 'Be still!' he commanded the waves.

Immediately, like an obedient dog, the winds died down and the sea became gentle and calm again. Jesus' friends could not believe their eyes. They could not understand what was happening. 'Look! Even the wind and sea obey him!' they said. 'What sort of man is this?'

Some questions based on the story:

◆ *What does the story tell us about Jesus' friends? (They were ordinary human beings who felt fear and panic. They saw Jesus as someone who could help them at all times. He was someone they could trust.)*
◆ *What does the story tell us about Jesus? (He was concerned about his friends' feelings. He had supernatural power.)*

JESUS HEALS A BLIND MAN

Based on the Bible story (Mark 10.46–52)

The streets of Jericho were crowded. There was a buzz of excitement in the air. 'Jesus is coming! Jesus is coming!' Everyone seemed to want to see this man. They had heard so much about him – and here he was, passing through their very town.

Bartimaeus could sense the excitement and hear the noise but he could see nothing. He was blind. He had been blind since he was born. He couldn't work so he spent his days sitting by the roadside begging. He too was anxious to meet Jesus, for he had heard of some of the wonderful things he had done – he'd heard Jesus had

Some questions based on the story:

◆ *Why was Bartimaeus excited that Jesus was coming?*
◆ *How did others treat him?*
◆ *Did Jesus treat him in the same way?*
◆ *What do you think 'faith' means?*
◆ *What does the story show about Jesus?*
◆ *How did Bartimaeus react after he was healed? Why?*
◆ *What thoughts might the crowd have had?*

healed people who couldn't walk, had cured illness and performed miracles. 'This Jesus must be a special man,' he thought. 'Perhaps he can help me. No-one else seems to care about me.'

'Look! I can see him. He's coming!' came a shout from nearby. The crowd pushed forward. Poor Bartimaeus nearly got trampled on. He felt so frustrated. He didn't know what to do. Jesus would never see him with all these people around.

'Jesus! Jesus!' he called at the top of his voice.

'Shh! Be quiet, blind man! Jesus can't be bothered with you,' someone said unkindly.
But Bartimaeus wasn't going to let this chance slip through his fingers. 'Jesus! Jesus! Help me!' he called again.

The noise of the crowd was deafening but Jesus could hear the pain and distress in Bartimaeus' voice. Jesus stopped and said, 'Call that man to me.' Bartimaeus threw his cloak off and stood up. With his arms outstretched he stumbled towards Jesus. People moved out of his way. Jesus looked at Bartimaeus with love and compassion in his eyes. 'What do you want me to do for you?' he asked kindly.

Without hesitation Bartimaeus replied, 'Sir, I want to see.'

Jesus said, 'Go. Your faith has healed you.'

At that moment something amazing happened to Bartimaeus. It was just as if someone had pulled some thick curtains away from in front of him. Suddenly the awful darkness that had surrounded him all his life lifted. His whole world was changed from darkness to light. He rubbed his eyes, blinked several times to make sure it was true and then leapt into the air with joy. 'I can see! I can see!' he yelled. He grabbed the nearest person and hugged them with happiness. 'Thank you Jesus! Thank you Jesus!' he repeated again and again.

The crowds looked on with amazement. They too could hardly believe their eyes! What they had heard about Jesus was true. This man really was someone special.

JESUS MEETS THE DISCIPLES

Based on the Bible story (John 1.35–42, Matthew 4.18–22)

One day Jesus was walking by the sea when he saw the fishermen Andrew and Peter. Andrew was casting his net to catch fish. Peter was busy cleaning and mending his nets. Jesus stopped and asked Peter how many fish he had caught. Peter paused and looked up catching Jesus' eyes. Peter immediately knew there was something special about this man.

Andrew came over and joined them as Peter told Jesus of their fishing trip. 'Yes – we've had a wonderful trip. We caught so many fish our nets were torn by their weight. That's why I'm mending these nets,' Peter replied.

Jesus nodded and smiled as he listened. When Peter had finished,

Jesus simply looked at Peter and Andrew in turn and said something rather strange. He said, 'Come with me. You won't be catching fish any more. From now on I will make you fishers of men.'

Both Andrew and Peter knew they had to accept Jesus' invitation, leave their jobs as fishermen, and go with their new friend. They knew their boat would be in good hands and looked after by the other helpers. From now on they had another more important job. They were going to help Jesus in his work teaching others about God.

JOHNNY APPLESEED

When he was a boy Johnny loved nature. He would spend hours in the woods and forests, studying the animals and plants. He used to love climbing trees and sitting quietly for hours watching the wildlife around him. Often Johnny would climb apple trees, and sit and munch the juicy fruit until he came to the core. Then he would carefully pick out the pips and pocket them. When he came down from the tree he would look for a suitable place where nothing else was growing and plant the pips so that new apple trees would grow.

When Johnny grew up his love of nature and wildlife remained. He used to wander around the countryside with a bag full of apple seeds. Children were fascinated when they saw him planting them. He loved to tell them about the beauty of the world around them and encouraged them to care for it the way he did. Johnny made lots of friends who gave him food and shelter. He was such a happy person that everyone liked him. They even began to call him Johnny Appleseed!

One night whilst in the woods Johnny became very ill. He fell down in the snow and could not move. Suddenly a great grizzly bear came by. He lumbered up to Johnny and sniffed him. Many people are afraid of grizzly bears, but because Johnny was friendly towards all animals the bear did not attack him. It wandered away, leaving its huge footprints in the snow. Later, some of Johnny's friends began to miss him. They started to search for him. When they saw the bear's pawprints they were worried. What if the bear had attacked him? Fearfully they followed the tracks. The pawprints led them right to where Johnny was lying very ill. Gently they lifted him and carried him back to where they lived. In the warmth of their homes, and thanks to their loving care, Johnny slowly became well again.

When he was completely better, Johnny thanked his friends for their kindness and set off on his travels again, planting apple seeds wherever he went. From time to time he returned to see his old friends who had looked after him. His fame spread everywhere. Wherever he went people recognised him and made him welcome. People knew him as Johnny Appleseed, the man who loved their country and made it rich with apple trees where once nothing else grew.

◆ *Ask the children what they think the main point of the story is.*

LORD KRISHNA

At Holi many stories are told about the god Krishna. It is said that he came to earth as a baby and grew into a handsome man. All the young women admired him even though Krishna loved teasing them and getting up to all sorts of mischief.

One trick he played was to steal the clothes of some milkmaids while they were swimming in the river. He refused to give them back for a long time and just carried on playing his flute.

Krishna was a good flute player. On another occasion some girls were dancing to his music. For a joke, Krishna began throwing red, yellow and green powder over them as they danced. They laughed and began throwing coloured powder back at him. Soon everyone was covered from head to foot with coloured powder!

MOSES AND THE TEN COMMANDMENTS

Based on the Bible story (Exodus 19–34)

The people of Israel had been travelling in the desert for a long time. It was hot and dusty and not a pleasant place to be sometimes. They often got tired and irritable and wondered when they would ever be able to settle down in one place. This time they were at the bottom of Mount Sinai waiting for Moses their leader.

'Here he comes!' someone shouted, pointing up excitedly to a small figure coming down the mountainside.

As he approached, Moses called out, 'Gather round quickly! I have got some important news for you.' There was a buzz of excitement as people wondered what it could be. 'Do you love God?' Moses asked them.

'Our God is a great God!' came the roar from the people. 'He set us free from slavery!'

'God has told me that if we do as he commands us we will be his special people,' Moses told them.

Together the people answered, 'We will do everything the Lord says.'

Moses smiled at their reply, and explained that God had promised to come and meet with them in three days, although they wouldn't actually be able to see him because he would be hidden in a cloud. Moses told them to go away and get prepared.

On the third day the people gathered around the mountain and looked up expectantly. Just as Moses promised a thick cloud appeared. Suddenly the skies thundered and the sound of trumpets filled the air. The ground shook. The people trembled in fear.

Moses, like the people, was terrified, but he climbed the mountain and was soon out of sight, covered by the cloud. On the mountain top he met God. God told Moses his Commandments, or rules, for the people, which were written on

(Background to the story. God had raised Moses up to be the leader of the Israelites. Moses had led them out of captivity in Egypt and across the Red Sea to freedom. After the exodus, there followed a very testing time wandering in the wilderness, during which God's special relationship with the Israelites was shaped.)

Some questions on the story:

◆ *What can we learn from the story about the Israelites? (They were fed up. They were somewhat fickle in their relationship with God.)*
◆ *What can we learn about Moses? (He was respected. He feared God. He was holy. He wanted the best for the Israelites.)*
◆ *What can we learn about God? (God cared for the Israelites. He wanted people to worship only him and to treat others with respect. He was forgiving.)*
◆ *What were some of the rules God gave?*

two tablets of stone. There were ten commandments altogether including the following:

> You shall not have any other gods but me.
> Do not kill.
> Do not steal.
> You should respect your parents.

The people waited at the bottom of the mountain for Moses. They waited ... and waited ... and waited ... but still he did not appear. In the end they got so fed up with waiting they even started worshipping another god, an idol which they had made!

When Moses did eventually come down he was carrying the two tablets of stone. He was amazed at what he found. He was furious with the people. He was so angry that they had started praising another god that he threw down the stone tablets with God's Commandments on. The stone tablets shattered into small pieces. The Israelites realised they had gone too far. They realised they had done something terribly wrong. They were very sorry.

The next day Moses climbed the mountain again and apologised to God. Moses asked God to forgive the people for what they had done. God did forgive them and gave Moses the Ten Commandments again. From that time on the Ten Commandments had a very special place in their lives.

THE MOTHER HEN AND HER CHICKS

There was once a mother hen who had five fluffy chicks. They lived on the farm. The chicks followed their mother wherever she went. They ran along behind her as fast as their little legs would carry them. Whenever their mother stopped, they stopped. Whenever their mother pecked, they pecked. They copied everything she did.

One day the mother hen and chicks were in the cornfield, pecking at all the fallen ears of corn. Suddenly the mother hen stopped and looked up with fear in her eyes. She had been startled by a crackling noise and the smell of smoke drifting towards her. To her horror she saw red and orange flames leaping towards her and her chicks. The cornfield was on fire! She knew she had to get away with her chicks. There was danger everywhere.

The mother hen looked this way and that, but to her horror found that wherever she looked their escape was blocked off. The fire was getting closer. It was no use running. There was nowhere to run. They were trapped! The mother hen was terrified, but her thoughts were not for her own safety – she was worried about the safety of her chicks. She could not let them be harmed. With no thought for herself, she gathered her chicks under her wings and made them lie still. The fire surrounded them.

Later when the fire had passed the farmer found the mother hen in the field. The farmer was very sad when he found that the hen had been badly burnt and had died. Gently he lifted up her body, but as he did so he heard frightened chirping noises and saw five little fluffy

◆ *When discussing the story stress the selfless behaviour of the mother and the fact that she was willing to give her own life to save the lives of her chicks.*

yellow bundles under her wings. Amazingly the chicks were still alive. The mother had acted as a shield and protected her chicks with her body. She had given her life so that her chicks could live.

MUHAMMAD (PBUH), GOD'S MESSENGER

Muhammad (pbuh) was not happy. 'My business is going well. My family are fine. So why am I sad?' he asked himself. He sat on the flat roof of his lovely home and looked down on to the bustling market below. Makkah was a busy city, full of people, but wherever Muhammad looked in the city he seemed to see nothing but greedy, selfish people. No one seemed to care about the poor and needy. Everyone always seemed to be fighting, quarrelling and stealing from each other. People believed in evil spirits and magic and worshipped many different gods.

Muhammad gave a deep sigh. All this made him very unhappy. He wondered if there was anything that would show these people how to live better lives and to give up their bad ways. Muhammad often spent long hours on his own praying and thinking about these things. Sometimes he would go out into the hills around Makkah to pray, where he could find peace and quiet and stillness. Sometimes he would go without food and stay for several days. One of his favourite quiet places was a cave on Mount Hira.

One cool evening Muhammad sat in the cave looking out at the starry sky and crescent moon. He was lost in thought. Suddenly he had a strange feeling he was not alone. Someone was in the cave with him! 'Do not be afraid!' a voice said. Muhammad rubbed his eyes and stared. He could hardly believe what he saw – it was an angel! It was the Angel Jibril.

Jibril showed Muhammad some words. 'Read!' he commanded. Muhammad was terrified. What could he do? He had never learned to read or write. 'I cannot read!' he stammered. The angel put his arms around Muhammad and held him so tightly that Muhammad thought that all the breath would be squeezed out of him. Just when Muhammad thought he would pass out Jibril let him go. 'Read!' the angel commanded him. 'But I cannot read!' Muhammad replied. Again the angel embraced him. After three embraces and three commands to read Muhammad suddenly realised that it did not matter that he could not read. He had a good memory and could learn things very well. So the Angel Jibril recited the words to Muhammad and he learned them by heart. Muhammad soon realised that God was giving him a special ability to remember all that Jibril told him.

This same thing happened to Muhammad many times over the years. At first, Muhammad was frightened by the angel's visits, but when he told his wife and others about the visits they realised God was using Muhammad as a prophet, as a messenger, to bring God's words to them. Muhammad was very excited when he realised that the messages were an answer to his prayers. The words the angel gave him would show people how to live better lives.

Some questions based on the story:

- *Why was Muhammad unhappy with the people of Makkah?*
- *What did he do about it?*
- *Why did he go into the hills to pray?*
- *What special thing happened in the cave?*
- *Why was Muhammad frightened?*
- *How do we know today what Muhammad said Allah told him?*

For over 20 years Muhammad received messages from God. He memorised them all exactly, word for word, and passed on to the people what God had told him. He told them to be kind to each other and to stop quarrelling. He told them to worship and obey Allah, the one true God. As people listened to him, some laughed at him, but others felt ashamed and sorry, and changed their lives.

Although Muhammad could not write, his followers wrote down the words God gave Muhammad exactly. They changed nothing. By the time he died, Muhammad had persuaded many people to believe and follow God's words. After his death, the writings containing God's words were all gathered together into one book, called the Qur'an. Today it is a book which is very special to Muslims, all over the world.

NOAH AND THE ARK

Based on the Bible story (Genesis 6.5–9, 17)

A crowd of people stood staring at Noah in disbelief. 'What on earth is Noah up to? Has he gone mad? What does he think he's doing – building a boat here? We're nowhere near the sea!'

Noah and his sons Shem, Ham and Japheth took no notice of them. They just carried on building the ark, which was like a huge boat-shaped house that would float on water. Noah knew something the crowd did not.

Since the beginning of the world the people on earth had got more and more selfish. They thought only of themselves and didn't bother about anyone else. God had given them a beautiful world to live in but they didn't care. They did not look after the things around them and just took whatever they wanted. God had had enough. He had given the people chance after chance to change but they would not listen. In the end God decided there was only one thing for it – he decided to send a flood to cover the earth and wash away those who did not live as they should. Only Noah and his family, who were good people, and some of each kind of animal would be saved. God told Noah to build a huge boat called an ark and to gather together the animals. He was then to wait in the ark where he and his family would be safe from the flood.

When the ark was finished Noah and his sons had a fine time rounding up the animals. The kangaroos kept jumping away, the lions kept growling at them and they had to wait till the crocodiles were asleep before they could catch them! At last all the animals were rounded up and put safely in the ark. Noah had taken plenty of food and water on board – so all they had to do now was wait. It wasn't long before the rain began. At first just a few drops splashed down, but soon the rain was bucketing down. It rained, and rained, and rained – and kept on raining. In fact it did not stop raining for forty days and nights. Can you imagine that? It rained so much that the whole earth was covered, even the highest mountains! There was nothing but still, flat water. The ark bobbed up and down gently on the surface.

After what seemed a very long time the waters gradually began to drain away. 'I wonder if there is any dry land anywhere?' Noah's wife said. 'Why don't we let out a bird to go and see?' 'What a good idea,' Noah replied. He took a big black raven to one of the windows and let it fly free. A few hours later it returned. It was tired out. It had been flying round and round continuously but could find no dry land anywhere.

Another week passed. Noah and his family were beginning to get a bit restless. 'Let's send a bird out again,' said Noah's wife. This time Noah chose a dove, but like the raven, after a few hours the dove returned, weary from flying round and round with nowhere to land.

Another week passed. 'It must be time to try again,' one of Noah's sons said. The dove flew off eagerly. In a short while Noah's wife shouted, 'Look! The dove is coming back!' Everyone crowded near the window to look. With a flutter of wings the dove landed back on the ark. In its beak it carried an olive twig. 'Hooray! Hooray!' everyone shouted. 'That means there must be land outside now,' Noah said.

A bit later Noah let the dove out again. This time it didn't come back at all. Noah knew that this meant that the water had gone down enough for the dove to find food to eat and somewhere to live.

After a little while longer the ark landed on the side of a mountain. Noah and his family fell down on their knees in happiness. They thanked God for saving them. 'We will always take proper care of the earth in future,' Noah promised. And God made a promise too. 'Never again will I send a flood to cover the earth. Whenever you see a rainbow it will remind you of my promise,' he said.

Some questions based on the story:

- *Why did God take such drastic measures?*
- *How would Noah and his family have felt before the flood?*
- *What would life have been like on the ark?*
- *How would the family have greeted the return of the dove with the olive twig?*
- *What was the promise God made to Noah after the flood?*

PETER DENIES JESUS

Based on the Bible story (Matthew 26.69–75)

Peter loved Jesus. He had spent three years with him and they were good friends. That very night Peter had promised he would never let Jesus down. Jesus had given Peter a strange answer. 'Before the cock crows tonight, you will say three times that you don't know me,' he said. Peter got very cross – he didn't believe that this could possibly happen. But when the soldiers came and arrested Jesus he just ran. He couldn't help it. He knew he should have stayed and helped Jesus but he ran off like a frightened rabbit.

Now he wanted to find out what had happened to Jesus. He followed the crowd until they reached the priest's house where Jesus had been taken. Peter went into the courtyard and stood by a fire to warm himself.

A servant girl passed by and looked at Peter as if she recognised him. 'Aren't you one of Jesus' friends?' she asked. Peter's heart beat in fear. 'No,' said Peter. 'I don't know what you are talking about.'

Then someone else said, 'I'm sure I saw you with Jesus.' Again Peter shook his head and said, 'I swear I don't know Jesus.'

After a little while another man standing nearby said, 'You are from Galilee, where Jesus comes from. I can tell by the way you speak. You must be one of his friends.'

'I tell you, I don't know the man,' Peter replied desperately.

Just then a cock crowed, and Peter remembered what Jesus had said to him earlier. Peter felt very ashamed. He had lied and let his friend Jesus down badly. Peter wept bitterly because of what he had done.

PRAHLAD AND HOLIKA

There was once a king called Hiranyakasipu who lived in India. He thought he was so special and important that he commanded everybody to worship him as God. Everyone was so frightened of him that they obeyed.

Hiranyakasipu had a son called Prahlad. Prahlad did not believe his father was God and continued to worship Vishnu. Hiranyakasipu was furious. He beat Prahlad severely to get him to change his mind, but it did no good. Next Hiranyakasipu got his soldiers to take Prahlad to a deep pit, fill it with poisonous snakes and throw him in. Many snakes bit Prahlad but he did not die. Vishnu, his God, had kept him safe.

Nothing Hiranyakasipu did to try and make Prahlad worship him instead of Vishnu had any effect, so the king decided to kill his son. One night as Prahlad lay asleep the king sent his elephants to trample all over him and crush him to death. The elephants did trample all over him – but they did not kill him. Vishnu, his God, had kept him safe.

Hiranyakasipu refused to give up so he sent a soldier to kill Prahlad. The soldier rushed at him and stabbed him with his sword. To his astonishment Prahlad was unharmed. His God, Vishnu, had kept him safe.

Hiranyakasipu was so angry he decided that the only thing to do was to use magic to kill Prahlad. The king asked his daughter Holika to help him. Holika was very special. She had been given a gift by the god of fire. She was protected from flames and could not be burned. Holika arranged for a big bonfire to be built. When it was ready she sat on the top of it and called to Prahlad to come and sit with her. Prahlad climbed to the top and sat down. No sooner had he done this than the king's servant ran forward and set light to the bonfire. Flames shot out and lit up the night sky. The fire burnt so fiercely that Holika's magic could not work and she was burned to death. When the flames died down Prahlad walked out of the fire. Not a single hair on his head had been harmed. Hiranyakasipu could not believe his eyes. Vishnu, his God, had kept him safe.

'I don't understand,' cried the king. 'How can you be saved by someone you can't see?'

'I may not be able to see Vishnu, but I know he's here,' replied Prahlad.

'How can he be here?' Do you mean he's inside a pillar like this?' Hiranyakasipu shouted, and hit a nearby stone pillar with his sword. Immediately the God Vishnu appeared as a roaring lion – and that was the end of Hiranyakasipu!

RUTH AND NAOMI

Based on the Bible story (Ruth 1–4)

Everyone was starving. There was no food in Bethlehem. Nothing grew in the fields. Elimelech, his wife Naomi and two sons decided that the only thing to do was to move to Moab, a far-away country, where there was plenty of food.

After a long journey the family began to settle into their new lives. It felt strange being in another country. The people were different. They spoke differently, dressed differently and worshipped other gods. However, in time the family began to get used to things. The two sons got married. Naomi became very fond of her new daughters-in-law, Orpah and Ruth.

But Naomi's happiness did not last long. Naomi's husband and two sons died. After a while Naomi decided she could no longer stay in Moab, and that she should go back to her own country.

Although Naomi loved Orpah and Ruth she told them they should stay with their own people and families in Moab. Ruth burst into tears. 'I love you,' Ruth said to Naomi. 'Please don't say I must leave you. Wherever you go, I will go. Wherever you live, I will live. Your people will be my people. Your God will be my God.' Naomi was touched by Ruth's love. She agreed to let Ruth go back with her.

Back in Bethlehem it was harvest time. The workers were busy in the fields gathering in the wheat and barley when Naomi and Ruth arrived. The women were tired and hungry, but Ruth knew she had to find food for them both. Ruth followed behind the workers and picked up the few bits they left or dropped. In this way they just managed to survive.

Boaz, the man who owned the fields, noticed Ruth and asked the workers about her. Boaz thought Ruth was very kind and unselfish to leave her own land and look after Naomi. He took a liking to Ruth and fell in love with her. Boaz asked Ruth to marry him. Soon she became his wife. Boaz also cared for Naomi and made sure she too had a home and food.

Some questions to discuss:
- *What did you think of Ruth?*
- *Was Ruth a good friend to Naomi? How?*
- *How must Naomi and her family have felt in a strange new country?*

THE SWAN

Prince Siddhartha lay on the neat lawn with his face up to the sky. A quiet nap in the shade of the tree was just what he needed after such a delicious lunch. In the beauty of the palace garden he could take it easy and decide what he would like to do for the rest of the day. Should he listen to music? Watch some dancing? Anything he wanted to do his father was only too pleased to arrange for him. The hardest thing the prince ever had to do was to decide what to do next. 'Life is good,' he sighed.

As the breeze cooled his skin he watched the leaves of the tree dance against the blue of the sky. He thought that he might stay in that quiet peaceful part of the garden all afternoon. He liked to spend time alone, but best of all, he liked to play with the animals and birds that lived in the garden. None of them was afraid of him. They knew this kind and gentle boy wasn't like the others who sometimes chased them and could be very rough.

The prince's sleepy eyes gazed as a flock of swans glided across the clear sky, but the scene turned to horror as an arrow, gleaming in the sunlight, spun upwards hitting its mark surely and swiftly. Helplessly he watched as the leading swan fell like a stone from the sky to land in the prince's garden. Siddhartha dashed over to where the injured and terrified swan lay on the neat turf. 'I'm not going to hurt you,' he said, gently scooping the swan up into his arms. 'Let's see what we can do with this cruel arrow.'

The swan seemed to know by the tone of his voice that no more harm would come to it while the prince was there. Though its wing was very painful the swan trusted the prince would know what to do. Gently he took hold of the arrow keeping the swan firmly on his knee with his other hand. A smooth twist and a sharp pull brought the arrow clear of the wing. The swan's pain began to ease, although a lot of blood was oozing out of the wound. 'I've got something that will make this feel better,' the prince said, pulling out a small bottle of lotion from his pocket. 'This wing will soon be fine,' the prince's soft voice sang to the trusting swan, as he smoothed in the lotion with gentle fingers. Siddhartha had won the trust and confidence of the bird and their friendship was growing when a sudden rustling of leaves and whooping of victory broke the silence of the garden. 'You'll never guess what,' Devadatta called running breathlessly through the nearby trees. 'The leader of the flock of swans. I got it! First shot!' Siddhartha saw the gleam of pleasure in his cousin's eye as he got near to him. 'Oh no!' thought the prince. 'How could he? Now there's going to be trouble.' Keeping a firm hold of the swan he stood up and turned to face his cousin, 'This is the swan, I'll bet.' A stony faced Siddhartha confronted Devadatta with the blood soaked bird. 'Hey that's mine! I shot the swan, so hand it over.'

The prince stood his ground, he had no intention of giving his friend up to someone who was likely to harm it even more. Tempers grew; Siddhartha kept hold of the swan even when his cousin challenged him to fight for it. Thinking that there must be another way of sorting out the problem, the prince suggested they went to the palace court. 'It's what grown-ups do when they can't agree over things,' he persuaded. Reluctantly his cousin agreed. 'Well, at least others will see my point of view. I shot the swan in the first place, everyone will agree it must be mine,' he called to Siddhartha as he marched ahead towards the palace.

In the courtroom some of the judges thought the whole thing was a waste of their valuable time. 'Two boys with a silly squabble,' they snorted. 'We've got better things to do than discuss who owns a swan.'

'Hold on a minute,' said one wise old judge. 'These children will one day be rulers of this country, they should learn about justice. A proper trial is called for here. Let's get ready to hear the two points of view and give them a proper verdict.'

Each boy was given a chance to convince the court that the bird should be theirs. 'I shot the bird, it should be mine,' Devadatta insisted. 'I found the bird, it should be mine,' Siddhartha argued. The court spent a long time considering the dispute; some agreed with one boy, some with the other. Then a strange old man stood up in the court and spoke in front of all the judges. They all took notice of what he said as he seemed to have an understanding that all respected. 'Life is the most precious thing of all,' he said to the agreement of everyone. 'So it seems to me that the swan should go to the boy who gave the swan life and not to the boy who tried to take its life away. Siddhartha valued the swan's life so he should have the swan.'

Put in that way nobody could disagree with the decision and the prince kept the swan. The king, the judges and his cousin watched as the prince took the swan back to the garden. Later, they saw him caring for the bird until it was well enough to be set free again.

DOROTHY VAUSE AND LIZ BEAUMONT

WHAT IT'S WORTH

All around Medina there was famine. Nothing would grow. People were desperate for food. Babies cried with hunger and mothers could do nothing to help. There had been no rain for months and people were starving.

One day the people spotted Uttman, an important leader of the community, returning home. His camels were laden with sacks of food. The people ran to meet him. They waved bags of money at him and threw themselves at his feet. They begged him to sell them food. Some even offered to pay him six times what the food was worth. Uttman shook his head and said, 'I'm afraid the food is not for sale. It belongs to someone who is paying ten times what it is worth.'

Later on that same day the people were amazed to find Uttman giving the food away freely to the poor! 'Who is paying for the food?' they asked. Uttman smiled and replied, 'Our Holy Book, the Qur'an, teaches us that if you do good to others, then Allah our God will reward you ten times over.'

ZACCHAEUS

Based on the Bible story (Luke 19.1–10)

No-one liked Zacchaeus. He was a tax collector and often took more money from people than he was supposed to. Zacchaeus became a very rich man.

One day there was a lot of excitement in the town where he lived. Jesus was coming! Zacchaeus had heard a lot about him and wanted to see him for himself. The trouble was that Zacchaeus was very small and would not be able to see over people's heads. Then he had an idea. 'I'll climb a tree,' he thought. 'Then I'm bound to see him.' So he climbed high up into a tree where he could see more easily.

Along came Jesus. As he passed under the tree Jesus looked up and saw Zacchaeus. 'Come on down Zacchaeus,' he said to him, 'I am coming to your house.' Zacchaeus was amazed because he had never spoken to Jesus before. He scrambled down from the tree and rushed home so he could welcome Jesus properly.

Some of the crowd began to grumble. 'I can't believe it! How could Jesus go to the house of a man like that! He's a thief and a crook!'

When Jesus arrived at Zacchaeus' house, Zacchaeus invited him in. Jesus looked Zacchaeus in the eyes. Zacchaeus felt as if Jesus could see right inside him and knew how bad he had been. Zaccheus decided then and there that he would change his ways and not cheat people any more. He said to Jesus, 'I will give half my belongings to the poor, and if I have cheated anyone in the past, I will pay them back four times as much as I took from them.'

Jesus just smiled and nodded quietly. He knew that Zacchaeus meant what he said.

Extra Background Information

Hindu Birth Ceremonies and Customs

The celebratory birth service is one of the important ceremonies (or samskaras) in a Hindu's life. But even before the baby is born, the pregnant woman may often read scriptures to the baby in her womb. Many mothers mark the baby with a spot of black kohl (often out of sight) to ward off evil. Also the baby's aunt may tie scarlet threads to the child's wrist or cradle for the same purpose. Later, if it is a boy, the baby's hair may be shaved to take away any bad luck or 'karma' he may have brought with him from a previous existence. A girl's ears may be pierced too. The exact time of birth is noted since a person's horoscope is considered important throughout life. A priest is usually involved in helping to choose the baby's name. Names chosen may be influenced by the child's horoscope, temple and family deities and names of other family members. As well as the naming ceremony, another important samskara marks the child's first outing. Then at around the age of seven a 'thread ceremony' takes place for some boys, denoting their move towards manhood. At this ceremony, the boy is given a thread of three strands which he must wear at all times from then on. At this family ceremony the boy makes promises accepting the duties of being a man.

Hot Cross Buns

These buns are made without yeast and can be made very quickly. This recipe provides enough for 10 buns.

Put all the dry ingredients for the buns into a bowl and mix with milk until the mixture is smooth and firm. Form into small balls and put these on a greased baking tray some distance apart. Flatten them slightly. Mix all the ingredients for the crosses and knead for two minutes. Roll out on a floured surface and cut into very thin strips about 5cm long. Lay two of these on each bun in the shape of a cross.

Bake for about 12 minutes in a hot oven (450° F, 225° C, Gas mark 7).

Ingredients
For the buns
100g (4oz) margarine
100g (4oz) caster sugar
200g (8oz) self-raising flour
150g (6oz) sultanas
½ teaspoon mixed spice
pinch salt
a little milk

For the crosses
25g (1oz) margarine
50g (2oz) self-raising flour
1 dessertspoon water

The Period Leading up to Easter

Shrove Tuesday is the day before the beginning of Lent. In the past it was a time to eat up all the good things before the time of fasting began. Traditionally people went to church to confess their sins and be forgiven (shriven). Interestingly, the word carnival derives from the Latin 'carnem levare' meaning 'to put away meat'. Mardi Gras also means 'fat Tuesday' and is celebrated on this day in some places. Pancakes are eaten. There are many pancake tossing and pancake racing customs.

The word Lent comes from an old English word 'lengten', meaning spring, the time when days begin to lengthen. It was decided that Christians should use a period of forty days before Easter to give up something they like very much as a reminder of the time Christ spent in the wilderness.

In some churches on Ash Wednesday, the priest marks the sign of the cross on people's foreheads with ashes which are a symbol of mourning.

Mothering Sunday is the fourth Sunday of Lent. In the past it was a time for families to gather together in their parents' home. Young people would take their mother a simple gift, such as flowers.

Seasonal Characteristics

- Spring: new life and growth, flowers and leaves emerge, buds on trees; young animals are born; birds make nests, mate, hatch young, migrant birds return; weather turns warmer.
- Summer: more sunshine; hot weather; longer days; crops ripen; harvest.
- Autumn: autumn colours, leaves change colour and fall; hedgerow harvest of berries, nuts and fruit; colder, crisper weather; mists and fog; days shorter; plants die back; animals collect food for winter.
- Winter: cold weather; grey days, frost, snow, ice; some animals hibernate; trees bare; plant some bulbs and seeds.

Simple Ideas for Making Books

- Making books may easily be linked to RE work, for example, re-telling stories, illustrating festivals, labelling activities, writing prayers, etc.
- Use different types of paper, for example, coloured paper, wallpaper, cloth, card, wrapping paper, etc.
- Books may be held together by stapling, sticking with tape, sewing, using treasury tags or loops of string.
- Covers may be made from different material to the pages of the book, for example, from coloured card. They may have pictures drawn, painted or done in collage, or they may be woven, or 'marbled'. The covers provide good opportunities for discussing titles, authors, illustrations, book 'blurbs', etc.
- Simple books may be made from four pages of coloured paper stapled together, consisting of pictures and captions or simple sentences on themes such as I like ..., I wish ..., I can ..., When I grow up ....
- Shape books, where the pages are cut into different shapes are another idea, for example, house, snowman, kites, etc.
- Zig zag (or concertina) books are very good for story writing in which there is a clear sequence of events. Once the story is drawn or written, the pages or drawings may be stuck on to a

long strip of paper which is then folded into a concertina to be opened out as the story progresses.
- Flip books may be made by stapling at the top or made with some form of ring binding. In these books the pages may be flipped over rather than opening in the conventional way.
- Cardboard box books may be made by covering a box with attractive paper and sticking pictures or writing on each of the faces of the box.
- Flap books are great fun. Individuals could make up a book of prayers or poems, pictures related to a story, for example, 'And this is what the snowman saw ...' . Whatever it is that the snowman saw is drawn and a flap stuck over it. Individuals could make their own 'flap' story or theme book or, if appropriate, these could be combined into a class book.
- Simple pop-up books could be designed as part of a technology project.
- Pocket books are another possibility. Simple pockets may be made from material, paper or card and stuck into a book at specific places, for example, 'Who lives here?' The particular animal or character is drawn and placed in pocket for reader to discover.

The Ten Commandments

These commandments summarise the most important points of Jewish law. There are many more detailed laws in the Torah and Bible. The Ten Commandments are:

1. You shall have no other gods but me.
2. You shall not make a carved image or any likeness of any creature; you shall not bow down and worship them.
3. You shall not utter the name of the Lord your God to misuse it.
4. Observe the Sabbath Day and keep it holy; you shall do no work on that day.
5. Honour your father and your mother.
6. You shall not kill.
7. You shall not commit adultery.
8. You shall not steal.
9. You shall not bear false witness against your neighbour.
10. You shall not covet anything that is your neighbour's.

Religious Festivals Chart

	Christian ✝	Jewish ✡	Muslim ☪	Hindu ॐ	Sikh ☬	Buddhist ☸
JANUARY	Epiphany					
FEBRUARY	Lent		Ramadan			
MARCH	Easter	Purim / Pesach	Id ul-Fitr	Holi		
APRIL					Baisakhi	
MAY	Pentecost					Wesak
JUNE						
JULY						
AUGUST						
SEPTEMBER		Rosh Hashanah / Yom Kippur / Sukkot				
OCTOBER				Diwali		
NOVEMBER					Guru Nanak's Birthday	
DECEMBER	Advent / Christmas	Hanukkah				

Many religious festivals do not fall on the same day every year, but move according to the phase of the moon or other factors, thus the dates on this chart are only approximate.

Songs

If you have *Sounds of Music* in your school, you may like to use these songs to support your RE teaching.

Sounds of Music song	SoM year	Sounds of Music song	SoM year
Alleluia	Y5/P6	I'm Gonna Sing	Y3/P4
Animals	Y2/P3	In the Summertime	Y1/P2
Autumn Leaves	Y1/P2	Join in the Game	Y1/P2
Away in a Manger	N&R/P1	Kite Song	Y4/P5
Baby Lying in a Manger	Y1/P2	Lazy Summertime	Y3/P4
Busy Farmer, The	Y1/P2	Lord of all Hopefulness	Y4/P5
Chanukah Song	Y2/P3	Now Light 1000 Christmas Lights	Y6/P7
Christmas is Coming	Y5/P6	Pinata Song	Y4/P5
Come and Sing	Y2/P3	Polish the Old Menorah	Y6/P7
Crossing the River	Y2/P3	Posada Song	Y2/P3
Dayenu	Y5/P6	Quietly	Y3/P4
Divali Song	Y6/P7	River, River	Y3/P4
Easter Bunny Hop	Y1/P2	Shadow Song	Y3/P4
Eternal Father	Y5/P6	Sing for Joy	Y4/P5
Evening Prayer	Y3/P4	Sing One Song	Y2/P3
First Nowell, The	Y5/P6	Sing Some Happy Song	Y5/P6
Five Angels	N&R/P1	Song of Thanks	Y1/P2
Floating in Space	Y4/P5	Sowing and Reaping	Y1/P2
Good Morning	Y1/P2	Thanks for Life	Y4/P5
Greensleeves	Y4/P5	Vesper Hymn	Y5/P6
Ha Sukkah	Y1/P2	When you Live in a Lighthouse	Y2/P3
Hark the Herald Angels Sing	Y5/P6	Winter Lullaby	Y1/P2
Here We Go Santy Maloney	Y1/P2	Winter Now is Gone	Y3/P4
I Saw Three Ships	Y2/P3	World Keeps Turning Around, The	Y5/P6

Sounds of Music is Stanley Thornes' primary CD-based music scheme which offers structured year-on-year progression from Nursery and Reception/P1 through to Year 6/P7. Clearly organised with comprehensive teacher support and specific help with planning, assessment and differentiation, *Sounds of Music* makes music straightforward to teach, whatever your own musical expertise.

For details please contact
Stanley Thornes Primary Customer Services, Ellenborough House, Wellington Street, Cheltenham, GL50 1YW, telephone 01242 577944/228888, fax 01242 253695

STANLEY THORNES infant RE

An overview of the coverage of the six major religions

Book 1

		General	Buddhism	Christianity	Hinduism	Islam	Judaism	Sikhism
UNIT 1: Myself	1 Who am I?	●						●
	2 How do I Feel?	●						
	3 At Home						●	
	4 My Family				●			
	5 My Day					●		
	6 My Friends			●			●	
	7 Jesus' Friends			●				
	8 Thinking of Others					●		●
	9 Belonging							●
	10 A Special Baby – The Christmas Story			●				
UNIT 2: New life	1 The Creation			●			●	
	2 Caring for the Environment			●		●	●	
	3 Hurt no Living Thing		●					
	4 The Seasons	●						
	5 Life Cycles		●		●			
	6 Growing Things	●						
	7 Babies				●	●		
	8 Holi				●			
	9 The Story of Easter			●				
	10 Easter Customs and Symbols			●				
UNIT 3: Special books	1 I Like Books	●						
	2 Telling Stories	●						
	3 Religious Books	●						
	4 The Bible			●				
	5 Jesus Calms the Storm			●				
	6 Jesus Heals a Blind Man			●				
	7 The Torah						●	
	8 Moses and the Ten Commandments						●	
	9 Muhammad (pbuh), God's Messenger					●		
	10 The Qur'an					●		

104

across Books 1 and 2

Book 2

			\multicolumn{7}{c	}{RELIGIOUS FOCUS}
			General	Buddhism	Christianity	Hinduism	Islam	Judaism	Sikhism
UNIT 1: Special times	1	Birthdays and other 'Milestones'	●						
	2	Harvest			●				
	3	A Shared Meal							●
	4	Names and Threads				●			
	5	Wedding			●				●
	6	Wesak		●					
	7	Diwali				●			
	8	Hanukkah						●	
	9	Id ul-Fitr					●		
	10	Advent			●				
UNIT 2: Special people	1	Special People in the Community	●						
	2	Anglican Minister			●				
	3	Jesus the Healer			●				
	4	Jesus the Teacher			●				
	5	St Francis			●				
	6	Moses						●	
	7	The Mu'adhin					●		
	8	Guru Nanak							●
	9	Guru Gobind Singh							●
	10	The Buddha		●					
UNIT 3: Special places	1	A Stone Circle	●						
	2	Special Places in the Community	●						
	3	A Place for Prayer				●	●	●	●
	4	Worshipping at Home				●	●		
	5	Cathedral			●				
	6	Synagogue						●	
	7	Doorways				●			
	8	Journeys to Special Places	●						
	9	Lourdes			●				
	10	Special Places for Buddhists		●					

STANLEY THORNES
infant RE

STANLEY THORNES
infant RE
Class Record Sheet: Unit......

Teacher .... Class .... Date ....

Lesson	Religious focus	Learning about religion	Learning from religion
1			
2			
3			
4			
5			
6			
7			
8			
9			
10			

This record sheet is designed for brief notes on opportunities for children's learning which have been developed during each Unit.